A Career in TV Meteorology

from the Best Weatherman Ever*

According to "the internet"

Alan Sealls

Alan Sealls

An Intellect Publishing Book

Copyright 2023 Alan Sealls

ISBN: 9781961485204 Paperback Ingram
ISBN: 9781961485358 Hardback Ingram

First Edition: 2023
RFV 9
www.AlanSeallsAuthor.com

Intellect Publishing, LLC
6581 County Road 32, Suite 1195
Point Clear, AL 36564
www.IntellectPublishing.com

Table of Contents

Alan Sealls

Introduction

E verybody has a story. Writing a book about your story is akin to delivering a weather presentation in that as soon as you are done, you lament all the things you forgot to include. That's why there's this revised edition! My story is about a decades-long career as a professional broadcast meteorologist. If you read the original book, Thank you. Thank you also for reading, period. Too many people gain their knowledge from USM. That's not The University of Southern Mississippi or University of Maine. USM is what I call University of Social Media, where professors are unknown people with unknown credentials and motives. In University of Social Media, people read a headline or look at a picture and develop an entire story in their mind, which is not necessarily factual.

In this revised edition of *A Career in TV Meteorology*, the original Chapters 1 and 2 are expanded into 5 chapters with a lot of additional material. The original chapters 3 through 9 are now chapters 7 through 13. Those are largely unchanged, with the exception of "Legal weather" in Chapter 9, and my "Final Thoughts".

In my story, I worked in multiple states and regions, at a superstation and at CNN, allowing people to watch me across North America and beyond. I saw myself on billboards, and I received recognition through several dozen local, regional, and national awards. I went viral on social media to be proclaimed "Best Weatherman Ever." It's on the internet so it must be true! Search and see for yourself. Many people call me a celebrity, but at home, I take out the garbage and cut the grass!

Not many people can do the job of a TV meteorologist, because it takes a perfect combination of skill sets, passion, training along with the right attitude. How many jobs are there where you give your professional opinion about something that has never happened before in the history of the universe, unscripted, to a live audience of tens or hundreds of thousands, multiple times a day, knowing that you could be wrong?!

This book is for those who are curious about all the wonderful, unique, enriching, strange, and worrisome experiences I've had in television. You'll find those mostly in the second half of the book. The first part of the book is mostly a career guide for broadcast meteorologists and for younger people who may be interested in broadcast meteorology as a profession. By way of my story, it covers what you give, what you get, and what it takes to succeed. My extensive career tips apply to all professions. The best career you can have is one in which you do something you love and get paid for it. If you do it well, the satisfaction is instant. The money follows. On the other hand, don't get stuck working just for money, in a job or career that is not fun and rewarding. We all have to do that at some point, but you just don't want it to be permanent.

Here's my journey… Enjoy!

Alan Sealls

REVISED EDITION

A Career in TV Meteorology

from the Best Weatherman Ever*

According to "the internet"

CHAPTER 1

Meteorologists

I am a meteorologist. A meteorologist is a person trained in the science of meteorology. A meteorologist doesn't just present the weather on television. In fact, most meteorologists are not on TV. Most meteorologists work for national weather services, armed forces, research labs, forecasting companies, private companies, and for universities as professors.

A typical meteorologist has a 4-year college degree in meteorology, which is also known as atmospheric science. The degree requires a solid foundation in chemistry, physics, computer science, and statistics. A year and a half of calculus is needed, too, before the student starts studying specific meteorology courses. The science of meteorology encompasses all of these disciplines, so the last two years of degree study focus on understanding the physics unique to weather. Upper-level students in meteorology learn how heat is transferred, how to read weather charts, how to forecast weather, computer simulations of weather, how clouds grow and interact, weather instruments, radar and satellites and their limitations, and how light interacts with air and water.

Meteorology students may take courses specific to agricultural weather, air pollution, winter weather, tropical weather, aviation weather, fire weather, atmospheric electricity, and severe weather.

Some meteorologists specialize in forensic meteorology — that's reconstructing past weather for legal cases where weather may be a factor. I've worked on multiple cases as a forensic meteorologist. In legal disputes or lawsuits, my role was to provide facts to help my side decide the best course of action in their claim or defense. Some of the cases I worked on were as simple as data collection and basic plotting. While other cases were much more extensive and involved.

One particular case involved the property manager of a rental beach home. A tropical storm caused damage to the property. The owner alleged that the property manager should have secured the house, given that there were alerts issued outlining the threats. The property manager claimed that they could not get to the property in time to do so. I was hired to develop a timeline of when watches and warnings were issued by the National Hurricane Center, and to document when the weather conditions began to deteriorate to the point that it would have been unrealistic to safely reach and then leave the property.

Another more-simple project I handled was pulling up the data from an ice storm for use in a case where a building owner alleged damage from the ice that an insurance company declined to cover.

I was also called on a dispute about wind damage to a structure installed on the roof of a high-rise. The structure had a wind rating of 130mph. A hurricane struck. The hurricane was not that strong but there were a couple of things that could have been factors in the wind actually reaching that strength. The first is that hurricane wind is recorded and referenced close to the ground. Tall buildings in hurricanes will typically have higher wind at higher floors. To estimate that, it requires using surrounding wind data along with radar data, hurricane hunter reports, and standard rules of thumb of the relationship of wind vs. height. The second factor is if the hurricane had spawned a tornado, it's possible that the tornado could have hit the building with wind over 130mph. Along with these scenarios, another variable is that the wind rating for the structure may have been for a wind gust of 130mph, not a steady wind of 130mph.

In addition to those I just mentioned, there was a case from a city in another region that was suing a company that designed and built a taxpayer-funded facility on a property that frequently ended up with standing water on it. The design company claimed the standing water was from rain. The city said it was due to poor design. My task was to pull rainfall records over an extended period and graph daily rainfall so that the city could see if the standing water happened when it had not rained. There was no rain gauge at the site, so I had to use multiple surrounding gauges, along with radar data, and satellite images to estimate what the rain would have been at the site.

Outside of forensic meteorology, other meteorologists compile weather data for estimating energy usage, or for efficient and safe building design in city planning, or for large construction projects. Meteorologists are found at large outdoor events, for public safety from hazardous weather. Meteorologists may do research outside or in laboratories in many locations around the world, or they may create weather models.

Some students go on to earn a master's degree, and then a doctorate in meteorology. Other students prepare for careers in broadcast meteorology. They practice and learn how to be expert communicators of atmospheric science to the general public. Broadcast meteorology combines art, performance, and weather.

The Occupational Outlook Handbook from the U.S. Bureau of Labor Statistics is an excellent resource to help you plan a career in meteorology, or any other profession. It outlines requirements, training, and salaries, along with a projection for the future. From the American

Meteorological Society (AMS), and the National Weather Association (NWA), you'll find listings of universities with meteorology programs, along with financial aid and scholarship opportunities. Use social media to locate student meteorology clubs at different universities and try to visit a local club meeting.

While meteorology is a fascinating, rewarding profession, know that meteorologists who forecast weather for the public, industry, or private companies, in particular, may have to deal with mental and physical stress. At work, have you been told to do less? Ha ha. I know the answer. Let's laugh together at that. Laughter is a good stress reliever. Have you been given shorter work hours and a raise? Okay, stop laughing. It seems that all of us work harder and juggle more tasks than ever. For a meteorologist, just creating an accurate and precise forecast or assessment on schedule can be stressful.

Big weather events are even more worrisome for forecasters. It may be long hours and many days of preparation and/or recovery. In the days beforehand, forecasters may be bombarded with the same questions, which don't yet have good answers. Even after a large weather event, there's the stress of swiftly completing an assessment. Storm impact can be costly, tragic, and deadly. If disaster follows, how might you handle it? Surely, you'd ask yourself if you did everything possible in communicating the threat, uncertainty, and possibility of disaster. After an immediate crisis, it wouldn't be unusual to experience sadness, guilt, and depression, to some degree. Combine those with stress from daily workload, and maybe from feeling overworked and/or underpaid, or from working in an environment that is unhappy, and you might need help. Those stresses, even without a disaster, can grow to critical levels. Stress and depression carry over from home life to job life and vice versa. They may lead to, or be related to, substance abuse. Our jobs certainly influence our overall state of mind. To be the best we can be as weather experts, and human beings, we must be aware of our psychological well-being.

- Wherever possible, limit stress. Avoid certain people who tend to have a cloud of drama over them!
- Maintain a regular fitness routine, which includes sufficient sleep and a healthy diet.
- Put time into a hobby or interest that has nothing to do with your job, so that you can let your mind relax.
- Whether you call it prayer, meditation, or just good vibes, stay strong spiritually.
- Focus on the good things and good people around you that you might take for granted.
- Prepare professionally with knowledge and training. You will be more confident and less stressed in most scenarios when you know patterns and possible outcomes.

- If you feel overwhelmed, reach out to friends and family; speak with your supervisor or human resources person; and if necessary, speak to a professional.
- Take advantage of counseling and mental health services offered by your company or agency.
- Find resources and support groups online for psychological well-being and for substance dependence.

We all have different tolerances for stress and anxiety, and different methods of handling them. If you are approaching your limit, don't ignore it, address it. Be well.

TV Meteorology

I am a broadcast meteorologist, retired. Broadcast meteorology is also called weathercasting. It is a mix of meteorology, computer science, and unscripted presentation. Traditionally, weathercasting was television and radio broadcasting. Now, it is multiple platforms, outlets, and variations. I'll still refer to it here as TV weather or just weathercasting.

More and more weathercasters are degreed meteorologists, but many decades ago, few were. Until the 1980s, most weathercasters were people who might have known a little about weather but were more presenters than scientists. It was common to refer to the "weatherman" on TV, as men dominated the profession. Since the 1980s, the TV industry has come to recognize the value of hiring people who are formally trained in weather and are excellent communicators. On the other hand, the TV industry broadly labels anyone who presents weather as a meteorologist. Just like engineer, chemist, or even minister, there is no legal definition of meteorologist. The title implies the person is formally trained, but there are many weather broadcasters who are not. The technology and data presented in a weather segment is now so automated that anyone who can operate a computer can put together a sequence of maps, and images with current and forecast data, and deliver a presentation, with little knowledge of what the data or maps mean. While that person could have the title of meteorologist on TV, they wouldn't necessarily be accepted as a meteorologist in a government or research or academic setting, or even in most other sectors of meteorology. I made that point to a TV station general manager, explaining why it was a stretch to call some of the weather staff meteorologists and he said, "I looked up the word meteorologist in the dictionary and it said it's a person who studies weather." He knew that calling someone a meteorologist would increase positive public perception. That dictionary definition lumps all weather broadcasters together, diminishing the backgrounds of those with formal academic or military weather training.

In addition to broadcasting weather information, weathercasters may perform other duties for their stations such as reporting, editing, photography, or web page or social media maintenance. Through their role as a scientist, they also become educators, public speakers, celebrities, and participants in charity events. The profession can be both challenging and rewarding in terms of personal satisfaction and financial compensation. Salaries for experienced weathercasters are good to excellent, based upon common standards. However, starting salaries for a college graduate are low, ranging from $28,000 to $35,000. The work hours are anything but "9 to 5," while job security ranges from solid to tenuous.

There are strict deadlines to adhere to, and the fact that weathercasters serve thousands or even millions of people by communicating information that can make or break a family outing or even save lives, adds to the pressure of the job. If you are ready for these challenges, as well as being subject to constant public scrutiny, then here are tips and things to consider in getting a job in weathercasting and surviving.

What name will you use? That might sound odd but consider that some weather broadcasters choose to use a stage name, or a name that is more easily pronounced or spelled than their legal name, while others choose a name that they think has a more sophisticated or exciting feel than their real name. Others avoid using a name that identifies their ethnic heritage, out of concern of societal acceptance. Some broadcasters don't use their legal name, simply to try to protect their private life.

What will your style be? It's best if it is something natural for you, rather than you trying to imitate someone else. Will you be a funny presenter, even if that is funny just in your mind? Are you a high energy, verbose individual? Are you a slow-talking, detailed scientist? Will you dress like a runway model, or will you be conservative in your attire? Whatever your communication style is, you have to cultivate it to make it attractive to a general audience, and to make you stand out from others in a positive way.

Develop a written resume, and a video resume, often called a "resume reel," where the word "reel" refers to film reels, used in early days of film and television. The written resume should include your work history, with emphasis on your background related to weathercasting, meteorology, and performing. With little professional TV experience, you'll want to include internships at radio or TV stations or in weather forecasting operations; volunteer work or classes at college or cable stations; and computer skills in graphics, audio and video, and web page or app design and use. Your resume video should be a short sample of your best work, because news managers receive dozens to hundreds of applicants. It could range from 3 to 5 minutes. Interns at TV stations may have access to produce mock weathercasts. College or cable stations may be available to produce a weathercast too. While green screen performance is an important skill, it's not mandatory. By the way, some TV stations use a blue screen rather than green screen, but blue eliminates a lot of wardrobe options! You can use a smartphone to produce a mock weathercast, with you standing in front of a big TV with weather maps on it. For those who really want the look, experience, and practice of performing in chroma key, there are several free virtual meeting and streaming apps that can create a chroma key, using a webcam.

Search online for TV broadcasting and weathercasting to find sites that also provide an enormous amount of information. Being able to find data such as addresses, phone numbers, or books is an important skill to develop. Read trade and industry magazines and online forums. Many are free and carry employment announcements. You'll also glean tidbits of information, like salaries in different positions in different cities.

Join professional associations such as the National Weather Association (NWA), American Meteorological Society (AMS), and Radio and Television Digital News Association (RTDNA). Seek out other science and journalism groups that might put more support emphasis on ethnic minorities or women, or under-represented groups, if that applies to you. Most offer a discounted or free job listing service. Some have a database of contact information for other members. Membership fees are typically reduced for students. Attend local chapter meetings of media and weather associations. Go beyond membership and join committees within professional organizations. You learn so much and you may make a name for yourself as an intelligent, involved, capable person. That leads to higher visibility, leadership roles, more material on your resume, and increased opportunity, while making your mark on the profession.

Network! Write to local weathercasters; many are happy to help young people. If you don't get a response, send an actual letter. That will stand out from social media and email. Keep in touch with your college instructors because they are sometimes contacted by stations looking to hire. Keep track of the contacts you make because you will see many of them later in your career. When meeting people at professional events, treat them as though they may be hiring you; managers can wear jeans and sneakers too!

Seek out a mentor but know that a mentor-mentee is a relationship that is best when it is natural. Just like a dating relationship, you can't just go up to a stranger and ask that they date you! You can't force it, and often times it happens without either side realizing it. A mentor is simply a trusted advisor who knows you as a person and gives guidance on your career. Most mentors are older people in your target profession, but they don't have to be in the profession, and they don't have to be older than you as long as they have experience in the path that you are taking.

A first-time weathercaster does not need an agent. Agents seek openings and/or negotiate contracts for 5% to 10% of your salary. Agents can't do anything for you that you can't do for yourself, as long as you are organized, persistent and resourceful. If you have the time and temperament for job hunting, and you don't want to pay commission, then do it yourself. The positive side to an agent is he or she is always looking out for your best interest and, ideally, he or she will have good connections for openings that may not be widely known; and he or she should have a better sense of what salaries are in specific markets or stations. For experienced weathercasters in larger markets, agents can be very useful but are still not required. On the other hand, television talent agencies and talent banks want a copy of your resume and link to your resume reel to show to TV stations. Agencies, also known as headhunters, keep a database and video files for stations looking to hire, at no cost to you (the "talent"). TV station groups often have recruiters who also keep a bank of resumes and resume reels of talent.

When you see a weathercasting opening, apply for a position by supplying a cover letter, resume and link to your online resume video. Most of these are now done electronically and online. Be flexible and realistic. First weathercasting jobs are usually in small towns far from where you would like to work, and the pay is low. Like many jobs, the salary has a pre-set limit in the station budget. It's very difficult to find out what that is, although some managers will be straightforward about it. Expect to work weekends and possibly use outdated equipment. You might have to work many months before you will be eligible for vacation or other time off. You likely will be assigned duties outside of weathercasting. If you are offered a contract, have an attorney or someone who knows the TV news industry approve it before you sign. Typical in standard TV contracts is an annual raise of only 2%, which does not keep up with inflation. Expect to have a probation period of 90 days with any new contract. Also, expect the contract to offer you little security. TV contracts favor companies, with things like a 60-day notice to terminate you for any reason, or 60-day equivalent pay to terminate you immediately. Once you sign, you won't have the option to walk away from the contract without financial penalty.

After you gain experience, it's not too difficult to land another job in a larger city. Keep in mind that for a listed job opening in a desirable city, there can be 50 to 100 applicants. If you send resumes to stations without a posted opening, many will not be acknowledged. Prepare for a lot of rejection in all job searches. If you are qualified and capable, don't take the rejection personally. In the first half of my career, my inquiries and employment applications were rejected by more than 160 TV stations.

Even when your work and ability is strong, getting a job always involves timing, something that you can't control.

Watch trends in markets where you want to be. Decide if you want to work in a weather-intensive market, a large market, a market where you can settle for many years, or the market that pays big bucks for a big personality. There are also opportunities in the companies that do state, regional, or national and international weather on cable, satellite, and streaming services. Weathercasters in those outlets have to be well-versed in geography. They may or may not create their own graphics, as local weathercasters usually do. A workday may involve more repetition than that of a local weathercaster, with some forecasts being recorded for later playback. These companies are competitive with local TV stations for salaries and benefits. In any case, be prepared to meet the challenges and know what you're getting into by talking to weathercasters who are there or who have been there.

If a station is advertising new positions, they may be expanding, and weather could be on the list. Openings often follow the sale of a station or a change in managers. Many stations post job openings on their corporate web page. Search online for sites that post jobs in TV weather. There is no one way to write a resume, or assemble a resume reel, or learn of a job and apply. Get information from many sources to arrive at a good consensus approach. Put emphasis on quality, not quantity.

Be prepared to "pay your dues." It takes time and good timing to move into the ideal position. Lack of formal training in meteorology will limit your options, although many successful weathercasters have learned weather on their own, and some are more knowledgeable than degreed meteorologists. Some TV stations require a meteorology degree and/or a broadcast certification, while others simply demand a good performer. The more education you have, the more options you will have, whether you end up on TV or in some other industry. For TV weather, along with general science, math, computers, and communications, you'll need to know a little bit about everything in life to be able to relate to your viewers and followers.

For a passionate weather communicator, the easy part of the job of a TV meteorologist is talking and teaching about weather and loving it. For many people, that is also the hardest part because there is no script. You may have an audience of tens of thousands or hundreds of thousands of people, and you must give a lot of information in a short period.

Some of the other downsides of being a weathercaster are that you are sometimes blamed for weather that people don't like; some people become upset or irate when you interrupt their program for a tornado warning; some people will be harsh on you; you lose your privacy; you have to work long hours and extra days during bad weather; you may be called in on your time off; your job may take you far away from friends and family.

Traditionally, TV stations have used specific months to measure how many people are watching, so that they could set advertising rates. Those periods are called ratings or sweeps. February, May, and November have been the key months, although more and more TV stations are getting away from that. For newscasters or weathercasters who work at a station that observes sweeps, they cannot take time off in those 3 months unless it's an emergency. For most of my career, that has been the case for me. I've missed a lot of family and social events.

What is it really like as a TV broadcaster?

Being a TV broadcaster is often embarrassing and odd. It's embarrassing to walk into a room, and everyone looks at you, and talks about you to other people, as though you are an exhibit. It's weird to go to a wedding and get more attention than the bride. It's odd to go to a funeral and get more attention than the dead guy. It's odd for strangers to know who you are. People often get too friendly with you, while others try to take advantage of your good nature and perceived wealth. Many plead for favors or help with some problem or project they have, that you can't control. You are looked at as the person on TV, rather than the full person that you are. It's frustrating when you are having a bad day or are going through something negative, and people disregard that and expect you to always be the happy, chipper person that you appear to be on TV. Visiting a friend in hospice, I was sad and uneasy at first but pleased to see how happy she was to see me. The nursing staff then recognized me and got excited. It was hard for me to smile and be happy with that; but when I realized that for them to recognize me as a friend of a patient might mean better care for my friend, it put me in a better mood.

Some people who recognize you will purposely be rude to you if they don't like your style or something about you, because they know you will not respond to them in the same negative and sometimes physical way that a stranger would. You are constantly under scrutiny and must be on your best behavior. Even when driving down the street, I've had other drivers notice me, and try to drive parallel to me, blowing their horn and waving to get my attention. Isn't that distracted driving? When I approach a stoplight where there are multiple lanes of stopped traffic, I make a point to never pull up exactly next to someone because they will instantly look at me. I stop either just ahead or just behind them so that my or their door and window pillars block their view! If someone else pulls up adjacent to me, I use my hand to partially shield my profile from view. I never look at them. I stop singing or talking to myself (everybody does that in the car, right?). I go perfectly still to avoid getting their attention. That's one of the many reasons why I love to travel. When I am in a place where no one recognizes me, I get to be a "normal" person. I miss simple things like riding public transportation without having to have a conversation with a stranger!

As a TV "personality," navigating purchases, or anything that requires getting and sharing information in a business setting, is filled with people who are distracted by who you are. They fail to be accurate or timely in the interaction or transaction, and they further distract you. I've been in stores where no clerk offered help until someone recognized me, and then mysteriously, every clerk in the store appeared to offer assistance. If you are going to give poor service to customers, be consistent. Don't single out people for special treatment! I was once in a store to buy a desk. I intentionally wanted an old, used steel desk because it was well-made and fit my home office well. The manager tried to sell me an aluminum desk because it was shiny and new and he thought I would want what is perceived by most people to be the best, but that's not what I wanted.

At restaurants, many servers assume you will leave them a big tip because they perceive you have a large income. I may have money, but I'm not just going to give it away. I'll give you a coupon, and yes, I use coupons whenever I can! I'm a saver. I once had a man contact me on social media, calling me names because several years earlier, he delivered a pizza to my house and griped that I didn't tip him or give him enough tip! I vaguely recalled that I either did not have change or I was distracted by guests, but a tip is earned. It is not a donation. Can you imagine someone holding onto that sort of thought for years, and then going out of their way to find you and call you a name, as though you are responsible for how their life turned out?

When you balance that with the good you do for people in helping them plan their days, safeguard their families, along with the positives of public education and community service, weather broadcasting remains a unique profession.

CHAPTER 2

Starting Your Career

For a career in TV, news directors want someone who looks and sounds good and can tell a weather story in simple terms. That will beat out any professional training by itself, BUT professional training gives you MANY more career options. In some television markets, you can't get a job without either or both AMS and NWA certification seals and/or a meteorology degree. Pure talent, passion and ability will get you far, but along with that, certificates, and meteorology degrees will take you further. If you fall short of the minimum qualifications for a job listing don't be surprised not to be considered.

Here are dozens of tips for weather broadcasters, especially those seeking jobs and trying to move up in the profession:

• Never send an unsigned or incomplete letter in an application. It shows that you overlook details.
• Never send correspondence with misspellings, especially when it is the name of the recipient that is misspelled.

- Never list references who haven't agreed to be listed. Once they agree, make sure they know when you are applying for jobs.
- Thoroughly research the station, the corporate owner, the station staff, and the TV market.
- Be prepared in an interview to do an on-camera presentation of the weather for that day.
- If you have a virtual interview and you are using a mobile device, make sure it is stable and steady. Ask if you should turn your camera vertical or horizontal.
- Don't dominate the conversation in the interview. Listen closely to what is being said so that you can have an intelligent response or follow-up question.
- On your resume and in person, be 100% honest about your credentials and what equipment you are proficient with. Just because you touched a computer a few times doesn't make you an expert.
- Asking no questions sends the message that you are not interested.
- Don't ask questions simply to appear interested. Ask questions for which you really want answers.
- If you are easily distracted in the interview process, it is a sign that you may have a hard time focusing on a daily basis.
- Just as in forecasting, don't be afraid to say, "I don't know."
- If you see something you don't understand, research it.

- Regardless of your degrees and certificates, you actually have to know what you are doing and be able to demonstrate that.

- Understand and embrace the technology behind how data is acquired, processed, transmitted and displayed. You cannot avoid it.

- Don't rely on a computer to do your job and don't rely on a model to forecast weather. When you do that, your value diminishes.

- Never stop studying and learning meteorology. Viewers and news managers expect you to be the all-knowing expert.

- As you interact with managers, ask what their preferred method of communication is. Email remains universal because of its flexibility and integration with other business software and the ease of including attachments.

- Be certain that when you and a manager set meeting times that you are talking about the same time zone!

- Before you call a manager, who is not expecting your call, stop and think about what the flow of their typical day and week is. Avoid calling on Monday mornings since that is when people have a lot of catchup or sudden work. Never call during or just before a newscast or severe weather.

- Ensure that your email display name is professional and the name you plan to use on TV.

- In your email and in your phone contact, use a tasteful headshot as a profile picture, so that your correspondence and you will be recognized. This is important once you join a company too, where someone else might have a similar name.

• Change your smartphone default email signature from "sent by my smartphone" to whatever you want it to be.

• If you use business cards, make them easy to read with large font, and a headshot. Add a QR code pointing to your professional website or social media or demo reel.

• Expand your job hunt. Seek opportunities outside the United States, in many English-speaking countries, or in other countries if you are multilingual.

• In weighing salary offers, account for the local cost of living, and whether, for example, the state has an income tax. It's possible that a higher salary will not yield higher take-home pay or savings and benefits.

• Whether you had an interview or were just able to get someone to give you useful advice, be sure to follow it with a sincere thank-you note.

• If you have multiple job offers at the same time, it is wise to not say no to any of them until you have said yes to one of them, ideally with a signed letter of intent! The worst thing that can happen is an offer you are about to accept is rescinded at the last minute.

These tips work for most careers, even though each profession may have different standards and protocols. When switching jobs, all of the above applies, but there are some other considerations:

- It's easier to switch jobs within your company than to get one in a different company. Your managers are more likely to support you.

- t's easier to exit a job when there's someone else ready to replace you. That's not something you control, although you might prompt colleagues and friends to apply.

- Anything you can do to help your company replace you will make your exit smoother, and it will result in positive references.

- Many jobs require you to submit a notice of intent to stay or to leave, with several months' lead time. That is very tricky since you often won't know for certain if there's another opportunity available.

- Don't misuse or abuse company assets or resources in your job search or at any other time.

- Give 100% effort until the end.

- When you leave a job, no matter how important you think you are to the company, don't be surprised if you don't get a big sendoff. Most companies don't like to make a big deal about people leaving!

- If you end up unemployed, continue to stay as professionally active as you can, on social media, doing public outreach, attending conferences, and improving yourself and your skills through online training.

- At conferences, dress like a professional. You want to look the role that you want to attain.

- At conferences, don't be shy. Strike up a conversation with a stranger and you may be pleasantly surprised at how valuable that type of networking can be. Even with meteorologists who are notable in the field, remember that your common interest in weather outweighs perceived glamor, achievement and job title!

I'm often asked, "When should a college senior apply for a job in broadcast meteorology?" The old rule was to apply several months before graduation. Now, companies are heavily recruiting meteorology students, taking the long view of tracking them through their college careers, offering them internships and fellowships, while building relationships years before graduation. These wise companies keep databases of students with potential, which include their graduation dates, and preferences for where they would like to work. Many of my former students got their first broadcasting job doing weekend-only work at a nearby TV station while they were seniors. This is an awesome opportunity for students, but the danger here is that the job may lead to diminished focus on academic life, especially if the station wants you to also do fill-in work, during the week.

If you are strong academically and able to balance a weekend-only job, then you can apply for a weekend TV job within driving distance anytime in your senior year. For full-time TV weather jobs that are hiring immediately, don't apply until your final semester. For full-time jobs, some stations, but not all, do have the flexibility to wait for the right person. If you apply for a job, and know that you won't be available immediately, you must make that clear in the application process, otherwise you create a bad name for yourself. If something prevents you from graduating on time, that will be a bigger problem! Definitely get job applications out when you are within a couple months of graduation.

The demo reel

Make a good demonstration reel. The first 15 seconds are crucial to your first impression. If the viewer doesn't get past that, the rest has no value! That means the very first thing on your reel has to show your personality. While many meteorologists are driven by weather extremes and weather with high impact, those are not what we talk about on TV the majority of the time. That's why personality in ordinary weather is far more important in most markets than how you handle a tornado. Show your face! You should be facing the camera in most of your video clips, rather than facing a side monitor. Eye contact builds trust. A warm smile draws people in. A sense of humor makes people want to keep watching.

A traditional demo reel has a short montage followed by a full weather segment. The montage is to show your different capabilities in chroma key, interacting with your anchors or reporters, covering live weather remotely, acting as a reporter, handling severe weather, while showing your different "looks" — formal, casual, etc. Don't let busy or animated graphics overpower your presence, and also don't dress so that you blend in with them. Everything on your reel must be quality over quantity. All video should be crisp, not blurry or pixelated. Start with a basic slate with a clean picture of you. Next to your picture, list your credentials and contact information.

On your demo reel, seek balance between science content and strong communication skills. Remember that clips in a montage are teases or samples, not full stories. Traditionally, a montage was between 45 seconds and a minute. Don't worry about a montage if you are new to the business and have little to work with. Managers understand. Something else students can include in a montage is an outtake of a map discussion or any public outreach or speaking where you are engaging your audience. Have a friend record video of it but make sure it is landscape (TV ratio) rather than vertical!

Separate the main weather segment from your montage with another brief slate. Your main weather segment should be one on an average day because no matter what market you work in, the majority of your forecasts will be average days. AFTER THAT, you can add whatever you want, like a full story package, or a severe weather segment. When posted to social media, turn off the option for ads in your posted reel since those are distractions and/or delays. Leaving ads active in your reel immediately tells a manager that you don't double check your work. Make sure that every element on the reel has audio on both left and right channels. At the end of your demo reel, you might include a QR code that links to your website.

Your reel is like a work of art in that there is no one way to do it and there is no magic length or quantity of material that is sure to get you a job! Perhaps what is most important to remember is that you are not creating it for fellow meteorologists. You are creating your reel for news managers to quickly decide if you might be the person that a viewer would want to watch every day. Don't assume that what impresses you will impress them. Get feedback on your reel from experienced colleagues and friends in the TV industry or in the communications department of your university, especially those who are not meteorologists. Since reels are online, you can post different versions to target the different markets or positions you might apply for, like those that may emphasize tropical weather, severe weather, winter weather or science reporting. Beneath or beside the video, if you are posting on social media, list what is on the reel and at what time it appears. Include a condensed or partial resume. Leave out sensitive information like your mailing address. Since anyone can make a perfect reel, know that hiring managers search online for any of your regular work; so, if you have anything old that does not flatter you, take it down!

Post good material online to your webpage or to a professional social media page that you'll use only for weather. Don't mix your personal life with your professional life. Keep your personal social media hidden from public view, but always assume it may be leaked to the public.

Students can do a mock weathercast in front of a big TV using PowerPoint or some other graphics and record it with a smartphone. It's not about chroma key, but it's about showing a manager that you have personality and weather skills. If you are bilingual, that is an important skill to list and display.

So many positions require reporting, so if you have any of that, put the best clips online, too, and/or go out and do stories with your smartphone about anything interesting and local like river flooding, clouds, the National Weather Service, gardening, or outdoor sporting events. Do a simple news or feature package that will also show you can edit video, and that you are resourceful. That is easily done on a smartphone.

Go to as many weather conferences as you can and network. More conferences are online or post material online. Online is great for knowledge but not very good for networking. At some weather conferences, there are sessions geared toward students, and opportunities to get critiques on your resume and demo reel.

For students, the American Meteorological Society also has a listing of internships, but you also do web searches for those, since some are listed in the same locations as jobs for TV. Contact TV stations directly to see if they have internships. Most TV stations list internships on their websites. Some internships pay, but many do not pay. For internships that don't pay, you will likely be more limited as to what you can do at the station.

Navigating jobs and contracts

Some TV stations require that the weathercasters have or earn certifications from the AMS or NWA. These certifications are known as seals. Each seal requires passing a written proficiency test, and a review of on-air presentations in which you are judged on content, graphics, and the overall ability to communicate science. Each one also requires that the recipient continue to learn and grow by doing things like attending conferences, taking online training, teaching, doing research projects, and staying involved with professional organizations. As you become eligible to apply for these, it's best to earn both, to give you flexibility in where you can work. Even if you never use them on TV, they will be a part of your resume and a part of who you are as a professional.

Once you get your first job, get the most out of it that you can. It is often a training position for the rest of your career. Don't take assignments as burdens. Take them as opportunities to sharpen your skills. When you think you are ready to move to the next job, don't try to break a contract just because you see something you like more. You should wait for your contract to end. Take the time while waiting to study, learn, practice, grow, and work on further certifications. There could be bad outcomes in trying to modify or break your contract. You run the risk of being known as untrustworthy in the industry. Your company or your agent may sue you for breach of contract. If you get someone else to renegotiate your current contract, then you could be breaching the contract with your agent, and you can be sued for that too. If things get negative with your employer or agent, then your reputation can be tarnished, even if you are being treated unfairly.

If your job lets you out of a contract for a non-valid reason that you give them, and then you show up on TV somewhere else, they will feel it was a scheme, and you'll definitely get a bad reputation and quite possibly a legal challenge. In any contract renewal or negotiation, it would not be unusual to go through several drafts of the contract to ensure the language and terms are agreed upon. I had one negotiation where a contract revision came back with a couple of key words surreptitiously changed, separate from the words that were supposed to have been changed.

Apparently, one of the corporate attorneys did that, and didn't tell the news director, with whom I was dealing. I noticed by using a trick I saw in an old black and white movie. I held the corresponding individual pages of the first draft and second draft up to a light, one on top of the other to see if any of the words shifted. Sure enough, a couple of words had been changed to give my station more control over my duties, which could have been detrimental to me. The news director was genuinely embarrassed because we had not agreed on that, and he did not catch it. Always read contracts thoroughly, and get an attorney, agent or other professional you trust to look over them too. Even if the terms of a contract seem unfair, if you sign it, you are agreeing to it.

I've had a dozen job contracts over my career. They have ranged from terms of one year to five years, with three years being a typical length. These contracts are also known as employment agreements, or personal services contracts. Most have similar components, arranged by section and subparagraph. Attorneys write them, so you will sometimes have to decipher legal jargon. For entry-level positions, contracts may only be a few pages long, with only the most basic terms. For seasoned veterans, especially for a higher paying and higher responsibility position, contracts can easily be over a dozen pages. In random order, here are common items you may encounter in a contract:

1. A definition of the two parties involved- you and the company. The company may be the owner of the TV station, rather than the TV station.

2. A definition of the term or length of the contract.

3. Salary or compensation for each year of the contract.

4. Description of the position and duties. Typically, this will be specific to your title, such as weekend meteorologist. It may simply be meteorologist. It may also be vague, as in staff newsperson. You want it to be as specific as it can be to keep you from being moved from your desired position.

5. Probation period. This is typically 90 days. Within this period, the company can decide that you are not what they thought you would be and release you with no further obligation.

6. Benefits. Some contracts will state that you are entitled to standard company benefits as outlined in the company handbook. Others will give a brief overview of holiday time off, vacation time, health benefits, etc., and then reference the company handbook.

7. Physical appearance. You will be expected to maintain a respectable and consistent look in your face, hair and wardrobe. Any substantial changes must be approved in advance by the company.

8. Name, image and likeness. The company has exclusive rights to your name, image and likeness for marketing and promotions for the term of the contract.

9. Statement of political neutrality. You cannot run for political office or publicly support a political candidate or party.

10. Non-disclosure of proprietary information. You cannot share company secrets or plans, especially those that would cause the company to lose money.

11. Non-disparagement of company. You cannot publicly say anything negative about the company. Even if you say it in private, and someone else makes it public, that is a violation.

12. Assignability. The contract can be assigned by your company to a new owner or a new partner, but you cannot assign your obligation to anyone else.

13. Copyright ownership or work for hire. Everything you create as an employee belongs to the company. You get no further compensation, and you can't claim ownership.

14. Exclusivity. You cannot do work for a third party that is similar to the work you do for your company. You can request in writing exceptions for approval.

15. No conflict with services. You cannot do anything that competes with the services that your company offers, or that takes away from their ability to generate revenue.

16. No owner of large share of competing service. You cannot be a large shareholder or owner of a company that competes with yours.

17. Company policies. You must follow all company policies as described in the employee handbook, or you will be terminated.

18. Right of first negotiation. Toward the end of your contract, you must announce your intent to renew or not renew your contract, giving your company the right to negotiate with you before other companies do. You cannot have discussions with other prospective employers before this point.

19. Right of last refusal. At the end of your contract, if you get a great job offer from another company, you must present it in writing to your company and give them the right to match the offer and keep you as an employee.

20. Opening mail. Your company has the right to open any physical or digital mail or communications directed to you, and then pass it on to you.

21. Suspended pay. This is a list of reasons for which you would not be paid.

22. Force Majeure and company disability. If your company faces disaster or extreme hardship and cannot broadcast, meaning they don't have work for you to do, they can end the contract.

23. Force Majeure and company disability. If your company faces disaster or extreme hardship and cannot broadcast, meaning they don't have work for you to do, they can end the contract.

24. Performer incapacity. If you become incapacitated and cannot work, you won't be paid. The company will have the right to have a doctor of their choice confirm you cannot work.

25. Termination. This is typically a long section listing the many reasons why you can be immediately fired,

which include creating public scandal, breaking laws or company policies, a criminal conviction, or failing to do your job. Typically, you can be released with no cause around your contract anniversaries, with only two months notice or pay.

26. Citizenship or visa status. You have to provide proof that you are eligible to work in the United States.

27. Non-compete. Upon separation from the company, there is a period in which you cannot work at a local competitor doing the same work you did at your company. It may range from six months to a year.

28. Payola. Payola is an old broadcasting term that means some entity secretly pays you or gives you something of value in exchange for you giving them positive news coverage or publicity. It is prohibited.

29. Breach of contract. If you do something which is against the terms of the contract, it allows your company to fire you.

30. Damages. Your company can hold you liable or sue you for the financial harm you cause to them by breaking a contract or violating some other rule in the contract. If you break the contract and leave, they can expect the cost of replacing you and even the balance of your contract to be paid back to them.

31. Buyout. A formula for the financial penalty you would pay if you were to buy yourself out of your contract. The amount is relative to your salary and how much time you have remaining on your contract.

32. Arbitration. Disagreements or disputes of contractual items are handled by a neutral third party, rather than in a courtroom.

33. Nonpayment to agents. The company has no financial obligation to your agent or representatives.

34. Union agreement. If your station staff is or becomes unionized, the union contract may supersede some items in your company contract.

35. Severance. For a typical TV weather job, this will state that you get no further compensation when you leave the company permanently.

We all want lots of money out of any contract negotiation. The way to get more money is to have leverage, which comes from your training, ability, experience and achievements, and how many other job offers you have at the same time. This means that early-career candidates generally have little leverage and should not expect much more money than what is presented. In place of increased salary, try to negotiate for things like paid moving expenses, wardrobe, and makeup and hair care. Extra time off may be negotiated but be cautious in asking for extra time off on a first contract at a new job. A person hiring you does not want to hear that you don't want to work! You might ask for time off for professional development like training or conferences. Other items that might be negotiated are reimbursed educational expenses, professional dues and certifications costs, and even bonuses for earned awards or ratings increases.

CHAPTER 3

Growing Your Career

For early and middle career broadcast meteorologists, in particular, here are simple things that can strengthen what you do:

1) Watch your weather segments with no sound to study the graphics, video, lighting, and your appearance. Consider that deaf people have an entirely different experience of watching TV. Don't forget the "vision" aspect of television, and that of social media too.

2) Without watching your weathercasts, just listen to them for delivery, breathing, pacing, inflection, and grammar. You must be clear and interesting, without visuals, as though you are on radio. Many viewers are not watching you, anyway, they are listening while they are doing something else. Some "viewers" may be blind or have a visual impairment. Do you have a fear of silence? Many weather broadcasters do, and that leads to an almost continuous delivery of words, with no pauses. Don't do that. It's okay, and perfectly natural, to take a

good pause at the end of sentences to let the message sink in, while you take a moment to fully inhale.

3) Analyze your weather graphics. Have they been tested in a focus group? Ask your non-meteorologist friends and family to tell you what they see or what message they take from the visuals. Most graphics are pretty, but are they effective? Is consideration given to where you will stand? Lots of graphics have large banners with multiple elements, along with more TV station or forecast information, often at the bottom of the screen. This reduces space for the actual graphical information.

4) While each station tries to be unique in branding active weather, the variety of branding words and phrases simply confuses the public, especially those that are not regular watchers of your station. Every type of disruptive or hazardous weather already has a designation from the National Weather Service. Be sure to use universal descriptions for dangerous weather. Don't just call it what it is designated. Call it by what it means to the public.

5) Radar, satellite and weather watch and warning graphics colors are different from station to station and online and on weather apps. That confuses the public, so you should use legends and/or be verbally descriptive.

6) Meteorologists are not without blame in confusing the public. It comes about through rapid delivery, filled

with jargon. Meteorologists have to engage the viewer, not entertain themselves with graphics. Wet dry, hot cold. That's all people really want to know on a typical day. Give them what they want, not what you want to give them. After you give them what they want, give a bonus to make them smarter, more aware, or more excited about weather.

7) Know your audience demographics. Are you in a large urban area, with subways and high-rises, or is it an agricultural region with low population density of people who spend a good deal of time outdoors? What do most people do for recreation? Never assume all your viewers or followers are as you are. We who make a career in TV tend to be or become middle income. Not everyone has a fireplace, or swimming pool, or travels outside of the region, or is able to pay bills on time and stay warm in winter and cool in summer.

8) Seek and accept advice from professionals. Between family and colleagues, I've gotten pearls of wisdom that work. Be yourself. Don't try to imitate someone else. Get or periodically meet with a financial planner. For any career, you hope for salary growth with strong benefits. Add bonuses and investments and you'll quickly see that all of that needs to be managed for your long-term financial health. Don't fall into the trap of spending money to live up to an image. Impress people by your character, skills, and work ethic, not by your possessions. Live

within your means. Don't buy things you really don't need. Don't buy a luxury vehicle when you can buy a less expensive dependable vehicle. Definitely find a safe place to live but don't live in a neighborhood or facility that you really can't afford. Beware of falling into the trap of purchasing too many things on credit when you can't immediately pay them off. That goes for trips and vacations too. Your credit will suffer. Consider purchasing disability insurance geared toward your ability to perform in front of a camera. Talk to your insurance agent about excess liability insurance. It will help you if people try to sue you for reason or for no good reason, just to get money.

9) Bad publicity from social media can crush a career. Do not ever do something in front of a camera that you don't want people to remember or share. Better yet is to not do those things ever. Do not ever be mean or rude to someone, but particularly don't do it on social media. It will live forever. Nothing is secret or hidden. Do not do anything to get you arrested or sued. That will make you go viral in a bad way. Be on your best behavior. Control your image. If you've already posted questionable or unprofessional content, delete it now. Don't compete with people doing silly things for social media attention.

10) Be choosey in who you associate with. The wrong person will get you in trouble. Once you are on TV, you will get more opportunities for who you date, simply

because TV makes you visible; but also because it has a mystique and people perceive that you are special just because you work in front of a TV camera. That's not the type of person you want around you. You want someone who appreciates, supports, and loves you for who you are, not for what you do, or for what they think you can do for them. When I was single, at a club in my 20s, I recognized a young lady who worked at one of the schools I had visited. She seemed to have herself together. We were talking and I asked her what her plans were for later in life. She looked me in the eyes and said, "I want to marry a rich man." In shock, I backed away. She was being honest, but that was not the type of woman I wanted to be with. I had other women outright offer me many "things," but I was lucky enough to realize that if something is that easy, it's probably not worth it. Choosing the wrong partner may lead to headache, heartache, drama, and a lifetime of mental and financial stress.

11) Be extra careful with romance in the workplace. In many careers, we may spend as much time with our co-workers as we do with our families. Co-workers become work family. Particularly when you are young in your career, new to a city and single, you'll see how easy it is to grow close to co-workers, sometimes leading to a romantic relationship. Dating co-workers can work out and lead to long and strong relationships, sometimes with a lifetime commitment. I've seen it too many times, though, when it didn't, but not necessarily more times than people who

date outside of their workplace. The big difference is co-worker romances that end make working with the co-worker awkward, difficult, and sometimes painful. While you can't help who you are attracted to, weigh having a workplace relationship with all the negatives that could follow. Avoid dating a supervisor or a subordinate. Avoid dating someone in your same department or unit. Some companies have policies against that, not just because co-workers may look at it as one person having personal favor at work, but because an end to the relationship may make one person less productive. Can you imagine if because of budget constraints you have to fire your lover?! What if you are a senior employee and then your partner gets a promotion over you? What if they get laid off and you get a raise?! How would you react if all your co-workers criticize your lovers' work ethic? There are too many situations where it's difficult to keep your personal life separate from your professional life. The worst situation I've seen is when a couple has arguments or fights at work. Aside from the gossip that follows, those involved should be prepared to be terminated if fights become physical or disruptive to the workplace.

12) Develop a timeline projection for the growth you want. That is in regard to knowledge, skills, ability, where you work, what shift you work, and even your salary. You need a plan, rather than going into a business where you float aimlessly. That plan also has to tie into personal life

goals of possibly marriage and children. Every couple of years assess and reassess where you are.

13) Dress for your role. Every professional position has a uniform that is often practical but sometimes not. Firefighters wear gear to protect them from heat and smoke. Judges wear dark robes to convey power. Combat military wear fatigues to blend in with the environment. TV weather broadcasters wear clothes that work in chroma key, don't conflict with lighting, and allow them to wear a microphone and radio receiver. It takes money and time to build a wardrobe. Students and those on a budget should start at thrift stores and resale shops, and then everyone should always follow the seasonal cycles of clothing sales. Don't pay full price if you can get something at a discount. Halfway through my career, I discovered that custom clothing is not as expensive as some people might think. There are now a wide variety of online stores that you can send your measurements to and order custom shirts, suits, dresses and even shoes.

Wool suits are best for men. Wool comes in different weights so that it can be worn all year in many markets. A cotton/polyester blend shirt is easier to maintain than an all-cotton shirt. Silk ties typically hang well. Ladies in dresses have to decide on sleeves or sleeveless. Part of that will be controlled by your station and by the weather or season. Clothing needs to resist wrinkles, and in many cases work for a person who is seated, not just standing.

For your work outfit, solid colors are safest, although some would say that's boring. Some colors and color combinations will be misinterpreted by viewers as you supporting an event, sports team, fraternity or sorority or even a political party! Be mindful of this when selecting your outfits. Never wear the same color as your chroma key! Any clothing patterns should not be loud or distracting. Avoid shiny things that will reflect the bright studio lights. White dresses and shirts cause many cameras to automatically darken the rest of the image. Keep a spare set of dress clothes at work, in case of emergencies. Similarly, keep casual clothing at work too, in case you have to suddenly report weather from outdoors.

Clothing has to accommodate TV hardware. Men wear belts so they are able to clip on a microphone transmitter and an earpiece receiver. Women often have to use a Velcro-type strap on their leg to do the same, since many dresses do not have pockets or belts or a place for transmitter or receiver packs. Sometimes, women secure those to the dress, on their back, but that doesn't allow them to fully turn their body to the TV or chroma key wall behind them. For women and men, wearing the actual microphone element centered on your chest or on your collar beneath your chin, rather than off-center, gives more consistent audio volume when you turn your head from side to side. For men, that means clipping the microphone element to your tie is better than clipping it to your lapel. Regardless of where the microphone element is worn, avoid allowing long hair or even a necklace to brush across it and create unwanted noise.

How much do you want the audience to focus on your attire vs. your eyes and expression? Do you want people to watch to see how you look, or to get the information that you are delivering? There's certainly a balance. Beyond earrings, face piercings and tattoos are more accepted in everyday life, but not universally accepted in the media. Be careful. Your desire to express yourself can quickly conflict with how a TV station wants you to be seen. Be consistent in your hair style and overall look. You don't want to surprise or shock the viewers, or your boss! In traditional newscasts, anchors were expected to be conservative. Facial hair was frowned upon for men (and certainly for women!). That's less of a concern now (for men). When aging, talent was expected to "manage" gray hair. That is also becoming less of an issue. Be yourself but know that more than most professions, your appearance as a TV newscaster has to be appropriate for the station and the community in which you work. An extreme example is that in some cities, women broadcasters are discouraged from exposing a lot of skin, whether that is arms or legs. In other markets, women are encouraged to show skin, and cleavage, because sex appeal sells. Is that what you want?

For men who plan to go far in television, invest in a nice tuxedo. If you become a high-profile person, there will be many events and occasions where you need a tuxedo. Purchasing one that is custom fitted for you will save you thousands of dollars in rental costs, over a long career. Society allows men to wear the same tuxedo or suit for years and decades but expects women to have a different dress for every occasion. It's not fair but it's the world we live in.

Men must care about appearance and wear clothing that fits well. A double standard forces women to have no clothing wrinkles or puckers, while men can be disheveled and get away with it. That's not acceptable. Common problems with men's professional attire are an "X" pattern wrinkle, where a jacket button pulls on a jacket or suitcoat that is too tight for the belly; jacket or suitcoat and shirt sleeves that are too short or too long; jacket or suitcoat collars that leave a gap on one side of the neck; shirts with weak or wrinkled collars; and ties with weak knots. How many men have their tie tip showing beneath the suitcoat, near the pants zipper? If it's unintentional, fix it by buying shorter ties, using a tie knot that shortens the tie, or by getting jackets and suitcoats that do not open up as much beneath the front buttons. Search online or ask a tailor for their opinion on how dress clothing should fit you. You'll learn a lot.

I've always washed and pressed my own shirts. I'm picky. It's not an enjoyable task, but there are a few practical reasons why I did so. The cost savings were significant over time. It meant one less place where I had to go in public and conduct transactions where people get nosey and want to see your stuff. In my experience, most dry cleaners are inconsistent in how they press clothing. Since it's something they do in bulk, they don't take the time to perfectly match the existing creases, so that you may end up with multiple marks where creases used to be. They may also over-press things that only need a light press, weakening the fabric, melting and cracking buttons, and sometimes leaving a permanent sheen.

My preference was to have at least two weeks of clothing on standby. In doing so, by late-career, I accumulated about 25 dress shirts. Yes, that's a lot, but the downside of washing and drying shirts is that they shrink a bit over time. Every few years I would order new shirts. My shirts were spread among the pastel or light colors of pink, blue, lavender, and gray.

You may be wondering what my suit and tie count was. In my mid-career, I had 17 suits, and over 60 ties. Suits and ties were hung in my closet in the order that I wore them, so that I could be sure my clothing combinations would not repeat frequently. Working 5 days a week, I could go a couple of months without wearing the same tie. There were times when I worked stretches of 11 days or more, so I didn't want to spend time trying to remember when I last wore something. Only a few viewers might notice or care, but that was just my picky goal. Over time, I realized that half of my ties looked the same on camera, so I lowered the number to about 35. I eventually embraced quality over quantity, so I got rid of items that didn't fit well or work well on-camera. It's tough to let things go that you like! What's in your closet?!

Hired, fired or maybe tired

As you go through your career, no matter how good you are or how well-liked you are, know that you are replaceable, and one day you will be replaced. If objective feedback, ratings and awards put you above the rest, remain humble. Especially when it comes time to sign or renew a contract, how you value yourself is not necessarily how the company values you. Be pragmatic in your expectations, but always do your best and continue to grow. Make yourself invaluable to your employer, which increases your marketability. Stay aware of job politics and unwritten rules.

In the digital world of TV, there remain gray areas. If you work at a TV station and see something newsworthy on your day off, and then record video of it to send to your station, are you working? If you are working then you should be compensated, and at the same time being covered by the station's insurance in case you are injured while recording the video. If you are not working, then you are the copyright holder of the video, but the station will accept your video and likely use it as their own. But what if no one asked you to record it? If you don't record the video, would your boss be upset that you didn't? This gray area can lead to disagreements and litigation. Be careful about doing things that you are paid to do, when you are not scheduled to do them or when you are using your personal resources! This is different from the expectation that you as a meteorologist will show up to work on your day off, when there's dangerous and newsworthy weather. That's a separate issue that can lead to conflicts and stress within your family or with your partner.

Weather broadcasters are somewhat celebrities and influencers, so job changes become newsworthy. As with TV news management, the tenure of some high value and high visibility meteorologists is sometimes short. This may not be much different from other industries where quick results in increased profits are expected. To the public, the loss of a local TV meteorologist to another station or city is sometimes like the loss of a friend. How stations handle that is critical since mishandling can lead to public disappointment, outrage, and an exodus of viewers. There are times when an employee is fired, or they get tired of the job and move on. In the mind of viewers, their favorite TV people can do no wrong. The viewers only see the curated image of us that we want them to see. They don't see us as our coworkers do. No matter where a person sits on the employee hierarchy, we are all human, with positive and negative traits, and sometimes those negative traits make us a liability to our employers.

It is always funny to see how management phrases the departure of an employee, in order to protect the company from a lawsuit, or from public backlash, knowing that the statement is often leaked to other media outlets by employees who may be unhappy with their own circumstances. Here's my interpretation of standard management statements when an employee leaves:

- *Join me in congratulating Bubba.* That means Bubba found a better job. He's a great employee but we can't afford to pay him enough to stay here.
- *Myrth has decided to move on.* That means Myrth found a better job. Either she's unhappy working here, or we can't pay her enough, or give her a good reason to stay here.
- *Jiff plans to spend more time with his family.* That means we and Jiff can't reach an agreement on his future here. One of us is being unrealistic. We think it's Jiff. While he job-searches, he'll probably be home more with his family.
- *Depi is no longer with the company.* That means we fired Depi or didn't renew her contract. Either Depi did something really bad, or we warned her too many times

about her work ethic or workplace behavior, and she has become a liability.

- *Do not let Frub in the building.* That means we fired Frub. He is a threat to the company and maybe to you. Watch out!

What do you or should you say publicly and on social media when you leave a job? It depends on the circumstances. The best departure is when you have a new opportunity, especially one that your old station can brag about, like when you get a better position at a sister station. The worst departure is one that is a surprise to you and to the viewers. When you suddenly leave a TV job that you feel you were forced out from, and you are upset, take time before you post anything. Whatever you are thinking of saying, run it by your mentor or close colleagues and friends or family first. Simply let the viewers know you no longer work at the station, although that was not your plan or goal.

- As hard as it may be, take the high road and thank your previous employer for the time you had there. If nothing else, thank your work family and the viewers for their support.
- It's okay in your statement to highlight a few of your achievements, as a mini resume for prospective employers.
- If you were forced out or feel that you were treated unfairly, NEVER air your displeasure online or in social

media. It's human nature to lash out when we are hurt by the actions of others, but telling the world doesn't help and it won't get your job back. Even if your perspective or allegations are accurate, you lower your future employment opportunities because no one wants to hire a complainer or someone who airs dirty laundry.

- If you plan to sue your old job, do not make public statements. Don't say or do anything that will weaken a legal challenge.

- Never destroy company property or shared files or do anything to slow the ability of your employer to replace you. While your feelings may be hurt, companies don't have feelings. They have profit goals. You will get negative references, even from the managers who once supported you. The company may also sue you.

- If you really want to make your old employer regret your departure and look bad in the public eye, go work for a competitor and succeed!

If you have a non-compete clause, that will place some restrictions on your next potential job. A non-compete clause is part of a typical contract that forces you to sit out for a period if you are leaving one TV station and going to another in the same market. In 2024, the Federal Trade Commission (FTC) attempted to ban non-compete clauses for most workers, nationwide. Some states had previously ruled they were unenforceable. The FTC's ban was challenged in court. As of this writing, the legality of noncompetes remains in litigation. The back-and-forth court challenges can be confusing and tiring.

In your job changes and career progress, use social media to your advantage. As you do on a daily basis, always weigh what you put into it with what you get out of it. There is tremendous pressure for people who work in front of a camera to have large social media followings. It can be a powerful tool in disseminating and seeking information or promoting a cause or a positive action or promoting yourself. Set boundaries for what you will and won't do on social media. Even on your personal social media, know that if you post something, and there's little reaction to it, it means it was not as clever, insightful or impactful as you thought it would be. Some weathercasters post daily weather maps on social media. If you only get a few likes on those, especially if it is just from the same handful of people who react to everything you do, but without shares or discussions, then your post is not interesting. Don't waste your time doing that every day. Quantity without quality is a waste of time and bandwidth.

The most effective social media post is one that gets many views or plays, to create conversation and then be shared. It takes a bunch of energy and luck to regularly create that kind of content. For your professional social media, you want it to relate to what you do, showing you as a passionate, credible, intelligent professional. We know there are many ways to get popular posts, but we also know many of them can compromise your integrity and professional standards. For weathercasters, the public loves to know about your personal life. Is that something you are willing to share? Babies and kids are always attention-getters, but babies grow up, and children need privacy. Pets are easy but when they become more popular than you, there's a problem! Do you really want the world to see the inside of your home? Would you put your hidden talents on social media? I guess it depends on what they are, and whether you truly are talented. Some people just do silly things to get attention. Others showcase their physical appearance. No one needs a college degree to do that.

Becoming a chief

Do you want to be a chief meteorologist? At some TV stations the chief is just a figurehead who has equal duties and responsibilities as the rest of the weather team. At most TV stations, the chief is the team leader, and sort of a middle manager who delegates duties and work, coordinates schedules, performs computer maintenance and upgrades, and sets the tone for how the entire weather team operates. Typically, but not always, that person has greater ability, training, and experience than the rest of the team and is paid more than others. A good chief is a leader, coach, listener, referee, teacher, enforcer, nurturer, and coordinator. A good chief shares workload and opportunity to create a strong team. A good chief follows the trends in the TV and weather industries, embracing technology and developments, and tries to innovate. A good chief is organized, detail-oriented, with excellent interpersonal skills, and ability to communicate, document, and ensure a smooth-running operation.

In my role as chief, I never asked a team member to do something that I would not do. I've filled in for team members on any shift, on short notice. I've also expected my team to take on my role and duties when I was out. I always wanted to see them grow, even if it meant they had to make decisions with bad outcomes.

I did learn something funny after a couple of decades in TV. I have right hand privilege. The majority of people, being right-handed, probably give no thought to left-handed people. The world is designed for us. In most weather offices, the team shares equipment in the same configuration. For computers, that means a mouse on the right side of a keyboard. After hiring a left-handed meteorologist who needed the mouse on the left of the keyboard, it struck me how unfair the world is to left-handed people. Not only did I embrace the mouse being on different sides of the keyboard when I started my shift, I actually started to use my left hand to operate it and reduce stress on my right wrist. That was just one practical side to accounting for and acknowledging our differences.

For me, being a chief was not an initial goal, but it was an inevitable one. My life's philosophy remains to be the best that you can be, at whatever you do, that is positive. Closely related to that is my belief that being the best you can be in your arena often means being the best in the arena. In that regard, I'm competitive; but it's a natural passion to just do better at teaching, sharing, and explaining weather, while mostly trying to outdo myself.

If you are considering targeting a chief position, remember in life you can lead or you can follow. Being the youngest of 4 sons, I was raised as a follower. In high school band, I knew I could never be lead trumpet because I wasn't good enough. I could read and write and execute but I had a very limited range. I played third trumpet. In fact, if there were such a thing as fourth trumpet, I would have been fifth trumpet! That's why I don't play anymore. I respected and admired the first and second trumpet players and was perfectly happy supporting them to contribute to the entire band.

That's what a news team is—a group of diverse players who come together to perform a newscast that was composed by a producer and conducted by a director. My part is the solo. I've always tried to deliver a memorable and engaging forecast, sprinkling in humor and conventions of metaphor, simile, analogy, alliteration, allusion, rhythm, rhyme, hyperbole, and personification. As a science performer on a weather team, I am the lead.

It's a situation where I'd rather lead than be led by someone who doesn't know where they are going!

A key lesson from playing in a band is if you hit a wrong note, you keep on going. You can't just stop and walk away. There are many days where in the middle of a presentation I've forgotten the name of a small community, or broken a grammar rule, or overlooked an important point I intended to make. Similar to an athlete who stumbles or wavers in execution of a play, it's how the game ends that sticks more in peoples' minds.

I'm not embarrassed to say that I'm an overachiever, because it beats the many people who are satisfied with mediocrity or being underachievers. Half of my drive is just who I am. The other half is intentional and deliberate. Be honest with yourself about your ability and your personality, including whether you are an extrovert or introvert, or even if you are uncomfortable talking in front of groups or a camera. Don't get deep into a career that is not a match for who you are.

CHAPTER 4

Weather Forecasting

Not all meteorologists forecast weather. Many do research or teach. Forecasting weather starts with an analysis of the current state of the atmosphere. One must know the temperature, humidity, pressure and wind at multiple locations and altitudes. That data, collected by weather stations, weather balloons, aircraft, buoys, satellites and radars is what's used to feed weather forecast models. The goal is to project how weather elements will mix and evolve to determine the future state of the atmosphere. The simplest forecast tells you when an approaching system will arrive. That's basic math as long as you know how fast the system is moving. Add on top of that whether it will be weaker or stronger or larger or smaller. The trends in the strength, size and even in the motion easily change. That's where weather prediction becomes more challenging.

AI or Artificial Intelligence is creating a revolution in forecasting. To meteorologists, AI has always been known as machine learning, where historical and current data is fed into computers which are so much faster than humans at finding patterns and connections. Artificial intelligence will enable much faster forecasts that are accurate farther into the future. It will also allow rapid updates on things like severe weather and tornadoes as they happen. Don't expect them to be perfect, though. AI models for weather also have limits based on the input data and our incomplete understanding of weather.

A human weather forecaster gains skill by years of making predictions. They learn to recognize local and global weather patterns that tend to create the same type of weather. Even with the aid of computer models, the human forecaster continues to improve by studying the latest research and techniques for predicting specific types of weather. Years of experience allow one to develop a mental database leading to quick pattern recognition, whether the pattern is one that covers large areas over several days, or one that is local, lasting just a few hours.

Glean forecast tips, methods and perspectives from others who may be more experienced in other facets of weather prediction, especially for scenarios that might be rare or new to you. Some of the best sources of forecast discussions are found online, in the various branches of NOAA. All local National Weather Service offices issue daily forecast discussions, as do the Storm Prediction Center and the Weather Prediction Center. The Climate Prediction Center has discussions for weekly, monthly and seasonal outlooks, while the National Hurricane

Center has discussions multiple times daily for named or numbered tropical systems.

TV weather broadcasters forecast weather and communicate it. In that regard, weather forecasting is an art which leads to a lot of public feedback, often positive, but sometimes negative or irritating!

"Weather is the only job you can get wrong every day and still keep." "The weather person just sticks their head out the window to guess at the weather." "You guys are always wrong." "I could do better." Don't think for a moment that those are my words. They are all sentences that cycle around like the Geminids meteor shower. They are also jokes that people tell me that they think I've never heard, so I laugh! Any place after a large weather event where the forecast misses the mark, those canned phrases are common in social media. I don't take it personally, even though some people actually believe the joke or hyperbole to be true. Others misinterpret a forecast or are using an old forecast. Don't plan tomorrow based on yesterday's forecast. Always use the latest forecast. I've even been blamed for forecasts from days when I didn't even work!

Where are all these negative pundits on the other 360+ days per year when the forecast is very close, if not right on the mark? How many times a year is the forecast really wrong? When was the last wrong one? Not many folks focus on the value of weather information on a daily basis to get people to work, school, appointments, and events without incident. Rarely is there praise for the thunderstorm forecast that helped safeguard kids on a soccer or baseball field, or the projection of storm timing that allowed drivers to get off the roads before a hazard formed. The overwhelming majority of weather forecasts in the United States are very good, thanks to research, study, and data. These are the forecasts that nobody comments on.

Is it going to rain? I'm asked that all the time. The question should really be, what are the odds of rain where I am?

Is this forecast I saw on social media true? I get that question every hurricane season from someone who sees a worrisome storm projection. A weather forecast doesn't have truth, it has probability! If the weather forecast turns out to be wrong but was based on quality data and solid meteorology principles, then it was not false, it was just wrong. Only the passage of time shows which forecast is closest to being correct. That means the question you should ask about a specific weather prediction is, "what is the probability of it being accurate?" The answer will be similar to that for the probability of your favorite sports team winning a tournament. You can look at all the stats you want, and listen to all the professional predictions, yet any one event can be decided by a single play which is not predictable. All forecasts are true, but true does not mean accurate. There is truth in the present and truth in the past but not in the future. The future has probability. The better question is how likely is this forecast to be accurate?

Meteorology is an evolving science where the public is so used to the forecast being right that when it is wrong, by whatever definition or opinion, it comes as a shock. When multiple forecasters in a given city get a forecast wrong, it's not due to human error or oversight. It's due to our inability to understand and sample the atmosphere.

What percent accuracy do you think your local forecasts have, 25%, 50%, 75%? They are more accurate than most other things that people attempt to predict in life. Can you predict where you will be and what your mood will be in exactly 31 hours, 22 minutes? This is something that is more in your control than weather. Go a week without checking any sort of weather forecast and see how many times you are inconvenienced by change. If you think back 60 days, how many times was the forecast wrong? The definition of "wrong" is your perspective based on your occupation and where you live and travel, but consider that weather forecasts are for a city, not your house!

Maybe you're not a meteorologist but you've seen one on TV. You are a forecaster, though, in daily life. How good are you? Every day you forecast your arrival time at work or school or an appointment. How does that work out? If you have kids, just getting out of the house on time is a forecast challenge. In your journey, you can't account for things outside of your control like vehicle problems or those bad drivers. It's always the other driver, right? How many accidents did you pass this week? An accident means somebody made a bad forecast in judging their stopping distance or turning radius or signal timing, or they just overlooked or ignored a traffic law. Maybe they under-forecast how long they could go before getting a mechanical issue fixed.

Do you play sports? How often do you miss the ball, whether you are swinging at it, kicking it, or catching it? That's a bad forecast. What about your goal or target? Are you anywhere near 100%? Do you go out of bounds? Look at the success rates of the best athletes and coaches. They are not 100%, and most are not even close to that.

You've bitten your tongue, right? How does that happen? Bad forecast. You can't blame anyone else. Have you had a relationship that just didn't work out? Ouch, that's a bad forecast. You are a human being, capable of mistakes, misjudgment, and unless you are a maximum-level-10th-degree-trained-in-the-woods-5-star-world-class-master, you mess up stuff that is within your control.

Why, then, is there surprise when a weather forecast is "wrong"?! This is not a defense of weather forecasters, but it is a reminder of why sometimes the forecast you get from multiple sources is wrong. Oftentimes, what people call wrong is simply an outdated forecast. A typical weather forecast has a shelf life of 12 hours. If you are planning tomorrow based on yesterday's weather forecast, you are not using the best data. That's because twice a day, there are two major sets of data gathered worldwide that go into computer models to generate new predictions. Planning the future based on an old forecast is like coaching a team in the final quarter of a game, the same way you started. Sometimes it will work, but more often than not, a coach has to modify strategy as the event unfolds.

We don't sample enough of the atmosphere because of limited sensors and sparse data. So much of our planet is uninhabited. We don't fully understand how air, sea and land interact with the transfer of heat and moisture. Computer model equations can't give accurate answers to something that is not 100% measured or understood. Computer models are like Hollywood animations—they look realistic, but they are not reality. They are guides, not guarantees. Our world is digital, but weather is analog.

How can we fix these shortcomings? Money! Investments by governments and businesses worldwide in increased weather sensing and detection technologies.

Educational investments in people with a passion to research and comprehend the workings of the planet, and then model them. Those will help, but they will never make forecasts 100% accurate. We've got a long way to go, to get anywhere near that.

So many times, I have given a forecast on TV or on social media, only to be followed with calls, emails, and questions of, "So, Alan, what do you really think?" For some reason, people think that I know something that I'm not sharing. That's never the case. When I give a forecast, I always focus on the most likely or most probable scenario, but then take time to talk about the best case and worst case. In communicating weather predictions, there are no secrets, just unknowns.

I've always created my weather forecasts from scratch, using raw data. That's how I was trained in my college programs. In my early career, I would spend hours analyzing data, before making the maps to show on TV. Now, my forecasting is faster because of the experience I've acquired of various weather patterns, and because technology offers more tools to help me focus on what's important. Some weather broadcasters don't forecast at all, and that's okay as long as they can communicate the science behind what is happening. They present the prediction from the National Weather Service.

Forecasting and covering severe weather

One of the largest weather forecasting challenges a TV meteorologist has involves severe weather and the hazards that arise from severe thunderstorms. Unique to broadcast meteorology is the requirement that you not only predict the severe weather, but that you simultaneously communicate it to thousands of people who are spread across a wide area. In large cities, you may be broadcasting to hundreds of thousands of people. The fact that a broadcast meteorologist is frequently on the screen with the data that she or he is trying to interpret, showing the data in a way that is acceptable to the general public, means that attention is split between forecasting and presentation.

For most TV stations, programs are interrupted for tornado warnings. Others will also interrupt for flash floods or severe thunderstorms. It depends upon the station management philosophy related to how frequently those threats occur in the area, and what the typical impact is. Like any other forecaster, the broadcast meteorologist has to know the local climatology for severe weather to be able to forecast it. There are weather patterns where you may only have a couple of tornado warnings over several hours. Those are cases where the meteorologist may be working alone, with no support. The more intense situation is when you have multiple back-to-back and overlapping tornado warnings, leading to long-form coverage. Those scenarios are typically foreseeable, allowing a weather team to coordinate and have multiple people working. A hurricane or winter storm leads to a slower, drawn-out version of severe weather coverage, but the preparation is nearly the same.

- You must know the science behind severe weather so that you'll be comfortable tracking, forecasting and explaining it.
- Coordinate with your newsroom and managers to ensure the news department is staffed appropriately.
- Set your home DVR to record your station so that you can review your work later.
- Get rest.
- Have all your severe weather graphics and explainer graphics ready.
- Refamiliarize yourself with all your available data products, computer functions, and the geography and pronunciation of communities in your area.
- Plan your wardrobe for items that are comfortable and practical since you will be moving around a lot.
- Secure water, snacks and food to carry you through the event.
- On social media and on TV, in the days leading up to the threats, give people preparation and safety tips.
- Tell viewers how they can watch your station or your platforms. Remind them that if they lose satellite TV

or cable TV, they can watch local TV with a regular antenna connected to their TV, for free!

- Explain how outlooks, watches and warnings are issued, what they mean, and what they don't mean.
- Put the impending situation in perspective by comparing it to past events.

When your severe weather coverage starts, ideally you will have another meteorologist with you, sharing all tasks, so that you can work as a "tag team." The Chief Meteorologist generally would be the lead, but many chiefs choose to give their team equal time. The positive of this is that each person can refocus more frequently and rest their voice, when alternating who is in front of the camera. Team coverage allows a person to take a break, get a sip of water and even use the restroom! It also allows everyone on the team to grow and to build trust with the viewers. The basics of covering severe weather on TV are the same for solo coverage or team coverage.

- Have spare batteries nearby for the microphones and earpieces.
- Let viewers know what signs to look for, indicating weather changes for better or for worse.
- Mention watch and warning thresholds and why certain locations are not under them.
- Remind viewers to take shelter anytime they think the weather is hazardous, even without a warning.

• Recap and summarize every once in a while, for people who just may be joining in.

• Be reassuring when possible, but also be honest about what you don't know or can't see.

• Match your verbal delivery to the threat level. Speech rate, voice pitch and inflection convey a lot of information, as do facial expression, body language, and even breathing rate.

• If critical data like storm tracks or polygons don't automatically update, you must quickly, manually create them.

• Occasionally, explain what the colors on a radar and all other maps mean.

• If you don't have a live radar, remember that fast-moving storms can be way ahead of where they are displayed on a close-view map, so think ahead when calling out streets and landmarks.

• Remember that visitors to your area won't know county names and most of the community names.

• Use tower cameras, live cameras and viewer video and photos wherever possible to show the active weather.

• When you operate radar or graphics for your partner, lead when you are not being led, since you will often have a better situational awareness than they do. That also prevents your partner from having to constantly tell you what to do.

- As much as you can with your partner, use eye contact and body language to communicate.

- Delicately correct your partner if she or he mistakenly says something on-air that's wrong, or hand them a note with the correction for them to mention.

- If there's a new alert or critical new data that your partner doesn't know about, and they are talking, politely interrupt, or hand them the information on paper.

- If you are on-camera, and your partner is doing a lot of talking, step out of the picture while they are talking.

- At any point of team coverage, if there is an unusually long period of silence, jump in and speak! Your partner may have lost their thought or been distracted.

There is a lot to remember in severe weather coverage, especially in markets where it is not common. All of that is on top of the real-time analysis and continuous short-term forecasting, multiplied by the number of warnings you may be faced with. As in many endeavors, to be effective, there are things you must do but it's sometimes just as important to not do certain things.

- Don't overexplain why something is happening, at the expense of saying what is happening.

- Don't refer to locations as "up there" or "over there" or "right here." Name them and use landmarks for reference. Talk like you're on radio, because some of the audience may only be listening, not watching.

- Don't talk weather lingo, using words like meso, echo, returns, pendant, couplet, vault and TVS. To the viewer it's a storm.

- Don't be afraid to tell viewers you will be silent for a short time as you read new information.

- Don't go more than 10 minutes without letting someone else speak, even if it is just briefly. You need to regroup and avoid unintended repetition and monotony.

- Don't block important data on screen with your body or graphic elements.

- Don't use a fast looping on radar when you are on a close view. Slow it down and shorten it.

- Don't use complicated graphics without a complete explanation.

- Don't use a composite radar on a local view unless you have no choice. Local radar will give better details.

- Don't forget that the radar shows what's happening above the ground and the details diminish as you get farther away from the radar site.

- Don't wear a white dress, or a white shirt if you expect to be in chroma-key without a jacket, because the camera iris may automatically adjust and darken the picture.

- Don't get tunnel vision where you stick to one message, while the data shows otherwise.

After the event, make notes on what worked and what didn't work so that you can improve next time. If you are able to archive some of the data and images, that may also be useful for later study. Look at comments from viewers on social media to get their feedback. A lot of it may be harsh, so brace yourself, but if you see a common criticism or critique from multiple people, take it and grow from it.

Personal weather

Everybody wants a personal forecast, right? You have one already in your weather app. The app fills in gaps that we TV weather broadcasters could never provide in 150 seconds. I share weather information and science that benefits all, but more and more people overlook the word "broadcaster," which means casting broadly. Social media may cause some to feel that we broadcasters are talking directly and exclusively to them. It is true that if you watch me on TV or your device, you let me into your home and space. Thank you, but I've never been there. I hate to break this to you, but there is someone else. In fact, there are tens of thousands of someone elses and each one would appreciate a personal forecast.

There's a perception that meteorologists have a complete and instant-access encyclopedia (that's like Google, but printed, and more accurate) of weather predictions everywhere. We don't. Most meteorologists forecast for a limited area. On our days off, we look at weather just enough to plan our personal lives and know if we might have to suddenly go back to work or cancel an upcoming vacation. It takes time and research to create a forecast that has value and accuracy.

Yet I am frequently asked by random people and family for a personal prediction. Asking for a personal forecast is like asking your mayor to personally let you know when the City Council votes on an issue for your street. Asking for a personal forecast is like asking a mechanic friend to listen to your engine and immediately determine why it is not running well, or asking an attorney friend if you have a case against a company that sold you a faulty product. Those professionals will tell you that they would need to sit down, gather data or measurements to make a diagnosis, and then try to figure out the answer. That's no different for weather.

What is different is if I were to put in the energy to generate a personal forecast, and then 12 hours later the forecast changes, especially to where you might be at risk of harm or financial loss, then I would be ethically obligated to tell you that. Multiply that scenario by the number of people who want a personal forecast, and you can quickly see how this would become a full-time, never-ending, non-paid obligation that would grow into a nightmare for me. I'm a good forecaster but I'm not as good as the forecasters in the place where you are going, or where your kids go to school, because they are there, with a local database and knowledge base that I don't have.

There has always been a small group of people who are chronic worriers or have a storm phobia who contact me when there's talk of strong thunderstorms or tropical storms. They ask me questions in the hope that I will tell them they will be okay. On a day with only one brief thunderstorm, that could be the one storm that knocks down one half-dead tree onto your house. For that reason, I can never guarantee that anyone will be safe. I've found that statistics and logic don't always reduce anxiety, and rarely do they cure phobias. The perception of potential harm from things you see coming is very powerful, compared to the unforeseen randomness of something like a vehicle accident. If you have a storm phobia, research astraphobia. If you don't see anything that sounds like a solution for you, then you must get help from a therapist or psychologist or psychiatrist. There is treatment that can give you a better quality of life, because there will always be storms. Be safe. Be calm.

Weather apps and websites provide more specifics and updates than I could ever give, locally or afar, even if I had time. Providing personal forecasts is not simple or reasonable for me to do. Sorry, followers. Sorry, friends. Sorry, family!

CHAPTER 5

Communicating Weather
Everyday words

There's sometimes a mix-up when meteorologists talk about weather because some of the words used in a technical context have different meaning in conversational English. It happens from poor communication by meteorologists and/or from misinterpretation by the public. Sometimes the mix-up follows spoken synonyms. I remember chatting with a co-worker about job contracts and I told him that a colleague had just re-signed. When I heard "reezined" come out of my mouth, I realized it might have been misunderstood. I restated it slowly as "re-signed" because there's a big difference between re-signing and resigning!

In 2005, when Hurricane Dennis approached the central Gulf Coast, the governor of Alabama was concerned there would be tropical drama in 'Bama. He issued a mandatory evacuation "for all of Mobile County and Baldwin County south of I-10." Was that all of Mobile County, and then only Baldwin County south of I-10? Was it both counties south of I-10? In that case, should "all" have been left out? A missing or misplaced comma changes the communication, as does where a pause and inflection are inserted in verbal delivery.

Effective communication is when the message sent is interpreted by the recipient as the sender intended. Here are some common areas where it takes some thought for a meteorologist delivering information to a mass audience:

A major hurricane means category 3 wind or higher. Can a non-major hurricane be a major problem? Yes. Category 2 Hurricane Sally was a major misery on the Gulf Coast in 2020. The word major used by a meteorologist has a technical definition, but major as an adjective is a matter of opinion.

A severe thunderstorm, to a meteorologist, means winds over 57mph, not just one that seems really bad. An enhanced risk of severe thunderstorms means severe storms are more likely than in a slight risk. Most people use "enhance" to signify an improvement, but that's not the case for storm threats. How many beauty products enhance your appearance? For some of us, makeup may be a desired upgrade that turns out to be a downgrade.

What about an upgrade? That's something we all want in our purchases. Doctors use upgrade to signal someone is in less danger, but in weather, an upgrade means the danger or intensity is increasing.

You may hear from a meteorologist that there's an elevated threat of flooding. Does that mean flooding is more likely in elevated places?! No, it means the threat has risen.

What about the normal temperature for today? That's not the normal we use in general conversation. The term "normal" used in weather is a statistical normal, virtually the same as the word "average." It does not mean that normally the temperature is a certain value. It means the temperature average based on the last 20 years of data is a certain number. Every decade, all the normal temperatures for the United States change. Normal rainfall changes too. It's no conspiracy. It is simply a routine recalculation based on more recent data. That data is different because climate changes, both naturally and through our actions. Think of the normal size of a house. Over decades, what we consider normal does change.

"They say the weather is supposed to be back to normal next week." That's what the woman sitting behind me said to her friend over lunch at the restaurant. Her friend nodded in agreement, "I'm tired of this stuff." As I glanced out the window at the puffy clouds hanging overhead, I wondered, "Who is 'they,' what is 'normal,' and 'supposed to' according to what law?" Immediately I thought of the number of times I've heard a fellow weathercaster say, "the rainfall is half of what it should be." Who says it should rain ever? It's no wonder that the public often expects something different than what is really forecast.

I consider myself a normal man for my age. But when I hear that the average man is taller and heavier than I am, I think, "Am I not normal? Am I somehow deficient?" No, even though some of my friends will argue that. In regular conversation we use "normal" and "average" to mean whatever is common or ordinary. However, in weather, these words describe the result of the common process of adding a bunch of things and dividing by the number of things to arrive at a mathematical average or normal.

In weathercasts, you'll hear something like, "the normal high for July 25th is 84 degrees." This means that the average temperature for that date is 84. It does not mean that the temperature is normally, usually, or even typically 84. Neither does it mean that the temperature should be or is supposed to be 84. It simply means that if you take the high temperatures for July 25th for the last few decades, add them up and take an average, you'll get 84 as the average or statistical normal. Most of those years, the actual high probably was not 84!

"So, what good is knowing a normal temperature?" you wonder. The average or normal high is a reasonable midpoint of a range of temperatures that we see on a given date. It is especially useful if you are involved in agriculture or in energy production or consumption.

Knowing the normals (averages) allows you to plan a season in advance. Gardeners have a guide on when to plant, while people can gauge upcoming utility bills. "But Alan, I'm not a gardener and I don't pay utility bills." In the heat of the summer, knowing if the temperatures will be above or below normal will help you predict your environment as it relates to people.

Those who love weather know that storms in the northern hemisphere spin counterclockwise, and high pressure has wind that flows clockwise. Consider that there are young people in our digital world who may never have used an analog clock or even been taught about them. They might not know what clockwise means! Similarly, generational changes in technology mean that the weather cliché, "broken record," meaning something that repeats over and over, will not be obvious to people who have never touched a vinyl record and experienced the needle skipping because of a physical defect. The younger your average audience is, the more you have to avoid references to things that are no longer common! You can always take the time to explain a cliché, but isn't the purpose of a cliché to save time and words?

When extreme weather is possible, no matter how fascinating you find the science, remember that the public is concerned and sometimes terrified of something that could change their lives, or even end their lives. Particularly on social media, temper your excitement.

Limit or cut out attempts at humor. Don't use an exclamation point on a social media post that conveys glee or giddiness. People will interpret that as you being insensitive. Approach it with the evenness of a doctor about to share bad news, but use language that the average person understands, not the traditional jargon of the profession. Communication is key.

Avoid using acronyms or technical words that we meteorologists use amongst ourselves. If you do use them and then take the time to explain what they mean, know that the audience doesn't care to be impressed by your knowledge in those moments. In everyday terms, explain to the audience what the threat is, where it is, how long it will last and what they need to do.

Can there be a "better chance" of a tornado? What's the "best chance" of a tornado? Zero! That's the way the public sees it. "Chance" is more appropriate for non-threatening weather. In conversation, people say "better" to mean greater or higher, but it's odd to use a word denoting positive qualities to something that is negative. Objectively, "a higher threat of a tornado" is a stronger statement. Even for rain, saying there's a "better chance for rain" would be more palatable in a drought, a situation where universally people want rain. I would never say "there's a better chance for rain" on a day when there are huge outdoor festivals and events, and people don't want rain. Just say there's a higher chance or higher possibility. Look at it as the viewer does.

A meteorologist might say that a tornado detected on radar is "impressive." Would a viewer watching that same tornado approach their house say the same thing? No! Are those intense storms "scattered in nature"? That's almost like when a police report has a suspect's vehicle as red in color. It's unnecessary words. The vehicle is red. The storms are scattered. Save words and save that brief moment when a listener wonders if you meant the nature of the storms is that they are scattered or that the scattered storms actually are occurring in nature.

In communicating weather, remember that there is confusion between weather words as nouns and weather words that are adjectives in regular conversation. Amongst ourselves, we meteorologists would casually say there's a "severe threat," meaning there's a threat of severe weather, something that has measured and objective criteria. To the public, that sounds like the threat is severe, not the weather is severe. As an adjective, severe is not quantifiable.

While the verbiage in a forecast might confuse, the one thing that should be clear in any language is the numbers, whether it's the wind criterion for a severe thunderstorm, a rain percentage, or the category of a hurricane's wind.

Always digest the numbers, along with the verbal description for the whole story. Many professions use words that don't make much sense to outsiders. For meteorologists, we've failed to consider how far our reach would be for those outside of our profession. Internet and social media have expanded our informal lexicon and our jargon. Slowly, we're working on it.

Those of us who deliver forecasts sometimes have another communication issue. Clichés that distract from the message. Clichés are a shorthand. Clichés are also like seasoning, a little is good but too much may give you heartburn. There's always that one presenter who uses too many clichés. What? No. Wait. Not me! Okay, sometimes it's me, but that's because weather is like a cliché farm. A successful weather broadcaster will learn to avoid clichés and speak in language that is colorful, yet original.

Weather clichés sprout and grow like weeds, although some are dry, and others are prickly, like a cactus. It is challenging to present live weather reports multiple times a day and creatively come up with words to describe the past, the now, and the future. It's a stormy relationship between science and prose, which prompts those with electric personalities to be lightning-quick, flinging a flurry of forecast findings, while remaining under the radar of redundancies.

Through the seasons of life, one never knows which way the wind blows, so it's easy to be clouded by mild-mannered individuals with warm thoughts, who may suddenly render a frosty stare, or the turn of a cold shoulder, when the heat is on. If you can't stand the heat, then stay out of the kitchen. The truth is, it ain't the heat, it's the humidity. Sufficient humidity makes rain and rain makes corn. Yes, I am skating on thin ice, when I point out that it may rain on your parade. Just stop, and smell the roses, because the sun will come out tomorrow. What a difference a day makes. Change is in the air. We will weather the storm! It's the price of living in our own little slice of paradise. What if something strikes like a bolt out of the blue, wreaking havoc? You may be flooded with fear, so turn around, don't drown. Into every life, a little rain must fall. Just keep your umbrella handy. As my mother once said to me, "Que sera, sera." When it rains, it pours. Too much rain is simply water under the bridge.

On another front, this is just the tip of the iceberg. Get your ship in the water. Climb every mountain. Leave no stone unturned in your quest for a quality forecast. Accuracy floats in the winds of change, particularly when all eyes are on the Atlantic, which is better than being in the eye of the storm. That's certainly no walk in the park, until you remember that every dark cloud has a silver lining, except for that twister that snapped trees like toothpicks, and sounded like a freight train. Was it a tornado? The answer is up in the air. This is a heated debate.

Have you had enough of this mixed bag? Was I as clear as a bell? We can put it on ice and enjoy smooth sailing and a ray of sunshine. Yes, much of this I pulled out of thin air. If you don't like the weather, just wait a minute. All we are is dust in the wind. I've taken you on a real roller coaster ride, but what goes up, must come down, down a slippery slope. By now, you are probably throwing some shade. I'll take the natural shade that comes from trees.

Slinging slang

Watch out for slinging slang. You may confuse people and even get yourself in trouble. In a broadcast, would you ever say, "snowfall amounts were crazy"? How about, "the winds are insane"? Is calling something a "monster storm" helpful for the viewer? There have always been generational differences in slang, as well as regional and international differences. An effective broadcaster takes that into account, when addressing a mass audience as well as the fact that new English speakers may take a literal interpretation of your slang. When in doubt, avoid slang, especially when the connotations may be X-rated!

What makes sense to you doesn't always make sense to others. Shortening sentences can lead to misunderstandings too. Returning from a conference, I called a cab from the hotel to take me to the airport. I wanted to leave at 5 pm. It was a small city so I had a sense that cabs might be limited. I asked the dispatcher for a cab at 5 pm. After a pause he said, "It's booked." I then asked for a cab at 4:45 pm, knowing that it's better to be early than later to catch a flight. Another pause, and then I hear, "It's booked." I'm starting to get concerned that I won't get a cab, so I asked about 4:30 pm. The dispatcher says in frustration, "Pick a time." Now, I pause, with the thought of hanging up, based on his rude tone. Then it hits me. He was communicating, "Your cab request is now booked," but I interpreted it as, "The cab is booked by someone else and unavailable." If he had said, "I've got it booked for you," there would have been no misunderstanding.

Call me a grammar snob, but I believe that speaking well allows you to economize your words and be a more effective communicator. English teachers cringe when people confuse "further" and "farther," and "there're" and "there's." If you don't know the difference, please look it up. In a professional setting, knowing which is correct in a sentence puts you a notch above people who don't. Broadcasters can never forget that a portion of their audience didn't learn English the same way as you did. There are many words we use out of tradition that are unnecessary and sometimes just plain wrong. Popular music makes dialects and slang acceptable, yet it's still wrong if you put it down on a college entrance exam!

Combine that with jargon for weather professionals and you end up with things like "heavy downpours." The definition of a downpour is a heavy rainfall. There's no such thing as a light downpour! We hear "heavy downpour" so often that it's not given a second thought. A downpour is simply a downpour, just like a tornado on the ground is simply a tornado. If a tornado is not on the ground, it is a funnel cloud. Don't get lost in the jungle of jargon. Use crisp, powerful language, where fewer words are often better at conveying a message than extra words.

Is it raining outside? Before you answer, take a second to know that if it were raining inside, we'd have a big problem! Rain only happens outside, but we tack on "outside" out of habit. Oh, the weather outside is frightful. That's a classic song lyric, but it would be even more frightful if the weather started happening inside.

There's another traditional weather phrase referencing barometric pressure. Air pressure is measured by a barometer. Why don't we say thermometric temperature?! For some strange reason, air pressure is the only weather parameter that we commonly speak of preceded by the instrument that measures it. When air pressure is falling in advance of a storm, you might hear that the barometer is falling. If the barometer is falling, then catch it. Those things are expensive!

In a windstorm, you are cautioned to drive safely with both hands on the wheel if in a high-profile vehicle. Is a high-profile vehicle a Lamborghini or a UPS truck? In most neighborhoods, a Lamborghini is a high-profile vehicle, but not because of its height! Most of your audience probably knows your intent when you say high-profile, but why leave any mystery? Just say tall or big trucks.

When a weather presenter talks about a storm moving away, you might hear something like the storm is moving north and east, but that would be a zig zag. It's more correct to say the storm is moving northeastward or to the northeast. As the storm departs, some would say it is moving on off to the northeast. If you delete the word "on," or delete the word "off," you end up with the same message. In fact, you can delete "on off" with no change in meaning. Why add extra words? That's similar to something like the storm will be gone in a short period of time. Delete "of time," or delete "period" and it still is a complete and clear message. Is *rain lagging behind the stalled-out front?* That sounds like something a meteorologist would say. Try, *is rain lagging the stalled front?* I just saved you two words that created redundancy.

"Safe haven" is a reinterpretation of safe harbor. A haven is defined as a place of safety or refuge. Have you ever heard of an unsafe haven or a dangerous haven? No. The word is more correctly used by itself as haven.

"Close proximity" is another phrase that is grammatically incorrect. Proximity is the degree of nearness, so you can say high proximity or low proximity, but close proximity is simply close. There's no far proximity, right?!

We get excited about the power and extremes of nature. Don't get bound by a limited number of superlatives. They lose effectiveness when overused. How often do you hear that something is incredible? Incredible used to mean something that was not believable. Now, incredible means something that is a spectacle or spectacular. Why not just use those words?! Is spectacular the same as amazing? By popular usage, probably yes, but when I think of a person being amazed, I envision them freezing, speechless and staring with mouth agape. How often can things be amazing and incredible before they really are not!

In weather jargon, meteorologists announce that "a new record has been set." If a record is new, then it is set. That's the definition of a record. You've heard the phrase, "past history." Isn't all history in the past? Yes. That's just like all warnings are for the future, making the phrase "advance warning" redundant. Beware the common phrases that are as redundant as PIN number and VIN number. In case you didn't know, PIN is an acronym for

Personal Identification Number, and VIN is an acronym for Vehicle Identification Number!

"We have a hurricane." That phrase uttered by a local meteorologist will raise the hairs on your neck. There's a problem, however, if the hurricane just formed in the eastern Atlantic Ocean. As soon as you say "we," you are implying that the hurricane will become our local hurricane. It's a critical distinction to avoid having viewers accuse you of hyping or playing up something that's not a threat. The birth of a new storm that is distant and not certain to become a local concern is more objectively phrased as, "another hurricane has formed," or "there is another hurricane." This is similar to a local meteorologist in Miami talking about computer models "bringing" a storm to central America. The word "bring" implies something that is approaching your location. Bring me that pen, bring me that book. If your cousin lives across the street, and you are talking to your brother standing next to you, you can't say, "bring that book to our cousin." You can say "take that book to our cousin." There is a case when a local meteorologist can say, "we are looking for a storm," and that's when a storm is moving from somewhere else to the state or country in which we live, since "we" would not be local. It would be regional. Even in that case, it's safer to say "a storm is heading toward our region" because a local audience expects "we" to be "we the people" in your local area.

"We are watching the tropics." That sounds innocent enough, right? It is except that from a local broadcaster, "we" could be the local community, or the TV station, or the community of meteorologists around the world. A local weathercaster can easily say "I" am watching the tropics and there's no dispute. What if they say, "there potentially will be a tropical storm"? That's not bad except it sounds close to, "there is a potential tropical cyclone," in which case "potential tropical cyclone" has a meteorological definition. Similar to "normal" high temperature or "severe" thunderstorm, more effective communication will avoid using conversational terms that sound like technical terms or vice versa, without clarification. Potential tropical cyclone is a lot of words that you might be tempted to abbreviate as PTC. Don't forget that PTC also stands for post tropical cyclone. Those two are on exact opposite ends of the life cycle of a tropical storm or hurricane, so there can't be any mystery. Sometimes you just have to say the whole thing!

I've always said that a good meteorologist puts as much if not more emphasis on communication ability than forecast accuracy. I credit that philosophy and practice with my dozens of career awards. Many TV meteorologists forget that "less is more" works in weather too. They have to remember to be a reporter, not a repeater. Repeating may make you sound credible, but reporting makes you credible. Reporting requires research. It furnishes reference and context.

There were two things I've done throughout my career that helped immensely with my communication skills. One was judging award contest entries in TV news and weather. The other was serving on panels to evaluate broadcast certification applicants for NWA and for AMS. This involved rating applicants' performance on objective criteria. However, there was always subjectivity. Most of the subjective perspective was averaged out by the diverse composition of the evaluators on the panel. We all think our own way is the best way, but certification criteria are more objective. Rating others in an application, or in an entry for an award forces one to look at oneself and ask, "Is it good because I do it that way? Is it bad because I don't do it that way? Do I do that? Why don't I do that?" Evaluating multiple candidates opens one up to unique and clever ways of effectively communicating. Similar to teaching, judging is a strong way to increase your ability to connect better with the audience. For both NWA and AMS, I later served as the seal Chair. The strength of that position is sometimes acting as referee, you are helping evaluators become more objective as you provide peer reviews for applicants who may never get another thorough assessment. As with all group projects, you quickly learn that not all panelists are as prompt or thorough as you would expect from a fellow professional! That is universal in all professions and endeavors. Sometimes those you think are sharpest are dull in some areas.

I still see the same presentation challenges and issues with not just early-career, but often middle and late-career weather broadcasters. In fact, I've been guilty of some of these too!

- Overuse of the phrase, "as you can see."
- Overuse of the phrase, "taking a look at."
- Pronouncing "temperature," a four-syllable word, as "temp-chur."
- Pronouncing "going to" as "gonna."
- Holding the remote with two hands and fidgeting with it.
- Holding the remote up constantly with one hand (a bent arm) for no reason.
- Not using both sides of the screen when available.
- Staring at side monitors rather than looking toward the camera.
- Stepping out of the frame but leaving your hands in the frame, pointing.
- Showing satellite or radar loops that are too fast or have a pause point that is too short.
- Looping a satellite image with fronts on it, while the fronts are not looping.
- Looping satellite or radar too many times with no stated purpose.
- Placing icons and features on maps but never explaining what they are.

- Showing a forecast animation that moves too fast and/or is too wide for people to see local details.
- Not stopping a forecast animation at critical and logical times, to point out things people need to see.
- Showing multiple forecast models and leaving it up to the viewer to decide which is best.
- Showing a forecast model that starts at a past time, instead of the current time or even more effectively, a future time.
- Showing an animated map, where stationary fronts move. They are stationary fronts for a reason!
- Using run-on sentences, or joining separate sentences with "and," "but," and "so," resulting in inhaling in the middle of sentences.
- Using acronyms and technical jargon without explanation of what they mean.
- Spewing large amounts of numbers without context of what they mean for everyday life.
- Assuming viewers know geography as a meteorologist does.
- Failing to teach the viewer things that make them smarter.

So, what's your physical delivery style? You'd better know so that you can fine-tune it. Some weather presenters constantly move toward and away from the camera. Others move in and out of the frame. Both of those are distracting when not done purposefully, and with limits. How do you gesture? Do you use one finger, two fingers, four fingers, an open hand, a back hand, a thumb? There's a time when any of those makes sense, but there are also many times where some of those make no sense! Watch others with the sound turned down to see if the pointing helps or hurts the presentation. Hand gestures also have connotations and other meanings so be careful! What about arm motions? Some weather folks present like they are guiding an airplane to the gate, or like they are a cheerleader with quick, synchronized arm motions. That quickly becomes distracting. Others use fluid motion like that in ballet or like someone practicing Tai Chi.

The graphics speak

You've heard the expression; *A picture is worth a thousand words*. By that old-saying, weather graphics speak. Some weathercasters use graphics without titles and legends and a verbal description of what they are, when they are valid, and what you should get out of them. A common graphic that is not explained is the outlook for severe weather from the Storm Prediction Center. Too often it's announced as such, but the public doesn't know (or care?) what the Storm Prediction Center is. Even worse, is that most TV stations show the graphic with a title of *Today*, or some other day of the week. The problem is that depending on what time zone you live in, and whether you are in daylight savings or daylight standard time, a version of the graphic labelled *Tomorrow* can be valid as late as after sunrise on the day after tomorrow. In other words, it's initially a 24-hour graphic that spans a day and a night. For a graphic labelled *Today*, the threat can go through tonight, past sunrise tomorrow, and maybe not even start where you are until late tonight or sunrise tomorrow. That is very confusing to the public.

Graphics provided by weather vendors, along with automated graphics are prettier than manual graphics of decades ago, but not universally better. Just because you can show these doesn't mean you should! Detail, clutter and the number of colors may lead to overdoing something that could be so much simpler for the viewer.

Do you have a problem with ALL CAPS in weather graphics? I do. Whether it is city names on a map or text on a graphic, some of us don't process all uppercase words as quickly as mixed case words. As a broadcast meteorologist, you are often given a graphics package, or a graphics look from your company that may not account for this. The graphics are designed by a graphic artist, approved by a promotions manager, and then used by a scientist to communicate to the public who may have little art and science and geography background. Ask co-workers and family which text style they prefer. Do a focus group on social media, and if you have the option to change graphics or fonts to what the majority of people prefer, why not do so? Your goal is to best serve the largest number of viewers or followers. That's not always easy when your company mandates specific things, like colors.

I once had a news director who had disdain for the color purple. He was the type of manager who saw himself as an innovator and visionary. When he first started at my station, he mentioned he didn't like to see purple in the newscasts. "Nobody likes purple," he said. "You don't see it on products in the grocery store." I didn't think much of it because he seemed to be thinking aloud. A couple of weeks later he asks me if I had taken the purple off the weather maps because, "The Weather Channel doesn't use purple." "What? You didn't ask me to do that!" I think to myself. The Weather Channel did use purple both on TV and online, but it was not visible much unless a very cold air mass moved into the lower 48 states. I asked the news director where he saw purple on my weather maps. He said it was in the temperature bands. This was in winter during an Arctic outbreak. Based on a standard color table showing the full spectrum of colors transitioning from one to another just as they do in a rainbow, he saw purple (violet) in the colors appearing in Canada and the northern United States. I tried to explain to him that you can't remove any one of the 7 rainbow colors and smoothly get to the neighboring color. "I don't like purple." He repeated. "Okay," I responded, "I'll tweak the colors." I made a slight adjustment on our master color table to narrow and put less emphasis on purple.

A couple of weeks later, the news director again presents his purple problem. He was not satisfied with my adjustment and tells me to call our weather vendor to see if they had a color table with no purple. I knew what the answer would be, but as a dutiful chief meteorologist, I called the vendor. They affirmed that they didn't have such a table. I report this intelligence back to the news director who starts his rant over that no one likes purple and then assigns me to check with sister stations to see if any were using color tables without purple. Here again, I knew what the answer would be. I followed orders and again, I was right. Everybody was using the same universal color table of which purple is a component. By this point, North America had warmed up enough that purple was not showing on the map. This was a lot of wasted time. If the news director had accepted that I was more trained and knowledgeable in my field than he was as a manager, he would have taken my professional perspective from the start. As I was walking past his office a few weeks later, he excitedly waved me in to look at a videotape of the previous chief meteorologist he worked with in a mountainous region. He bragged about how good the meteorologist was and how well he used graphics. The meteorologist was showing pretty temperature maps of the mountains and valleys. Within a few seconds of the presentation, guess what color shows up on the map. Purple! All the news director could do is softly say, "oh." That was the last I heard of the purple problem.

Aside from color preference, one of the big issues to remember is that some viewers are partially or fully color-blind. That's when map legends become more valuable. Even aside from interpreting color, you cannot assume that people who view your presentation are the same expert map reader that you are. When using wide map views in a local broadcast to show a broad overview, just for example, does it make sense to show highways? Would something like Interstates help local viewers know where a storm is across the country, or would Interstates just clutter the map? Don't just use the default settings that came with the computer system. Take control and have it tell the story you want to tell, with minimal distraction and clutter, while every element is purposeful and meaningful.

In hurricane season, many weather broadcasters almost become "hurricane coneheads." That's what I jokingly call people who put so much emphasis on the forecast cone for tropical systems, that they forget to focus on the actual threats. Some of the public then become "hurricane coneheads" too because they believe that the cone is the definitive tool to know where and when a system will strike. The impacts of tropical depressions, tropical storms, and hurricanes are always within and outside of the forecast cone for the first couple of days of the forecast. After that, the impacts may still be within and outside the forecast cone. "Coneheads" mistakenly think the cone is for impacts, but it is not.

If you plan to be any sort of decent weathercaster, you'd better know geography. Not just local, but regional, national, and global. People often get indignant if you misidentify a place that they know well. On the other hand, don't forget that many people have never traveled beyond a limited distance. That means you have to not just pronounce location names correctly, but you also must give a reference for where they are, or where they are near. In hurricane season, meteorologists often use references to the Lesser Antilles, or Windward Islands, or Hispaniola. How much of the public do you think know where those are? I did a simple Facebook poll asking people if they knew where Hispaniola was, and then the same for the Lesser Antilles. Twelve percent of respondents said they did not know, for each one. I would bet that the percentage of the public who do not know is much higher than that, but many people are unwilling to admit that they don't know something, especially on public-facing social media!

CHAPTER 6

Changes in TV Weather

Over my career as a broadcast meteorologist, there have been revolutionary changes in communication and technology and weather forecasting. When I first started in the 1980s, video was recorded on videotape on large, bulky cameras. The computers we used for weather graphics only gave 16 colors, in low resolution. To show a satellite image or radar image, we used a modem to dial up and download an image, one at a time. It was common for the microphone, earpiece receiver, and weather computer controller to each have long cables that made it difficult for the meteorologist to move around. If the public wanted to reach us, they called on a landline or sent a letter. Weather maps were printed on large paper, analyzed by hand, and hung on a wall. Weather forecast models only reliably went a couple of days out, with low resolution. Some TV stations had a service where you could call a phone number and receive the time and temperature and forecast!

In the 1990s, computers evolved to show millions of colors. Software updates were done on removable floppy disks. Data was delivered by satellite. We broadcasters could show radar and cloud satellite loops, and then show them in a three-dimensional perspective. It sometimes took an hour to generate a short three-dimensional satellite view that changed over time. Lightning data became available to display on TV. Wireless microphones, earpieces, and weather computer controllers became standard. TV stations began to acquire live cameras and remote weather stations. Some TV stations also invested hundreds of thousands of dollars into getting their own radar. Videotapes became digital. Email became ubiquitous. TV stations started websites.

In the 2000s, cell phones put data in our pockets, and cell phone cameras made it so much easier for people to document weather. TV station cameras transitioned from analog to a digital workflow. Streaming video services opened up the number of places where news and weather were seen. Social media grew and exploded. That created many sources of news, photos, and video for TV stations. The proliferation of cell phone cameras and social media made hoaxes and false information more common. I once fell for a hoax photo during a hurricane, and since then, I'm always skeptical about any photo that seems too good to be real. I later got a series of emails, with different email addresses, and various grainy photos of a supposed UFO in my area. The pictures were obviously from other parts of the country, and it turned out that the different emails were all from the same IP address. That one I caught!

In the 2010s, TV stations transitioned to HDTV, and became all-digital. Reporters could do live reports from anywhere, using bonded cell phone data transmission, instead of expensive trucks using microwave or satellite transmission. We meteorologists were strongly encouraged to interact with viewers on social media, on multiple apps, and in live chats. We could now access our work computers from home and do a large part of our jobs using cell phones remotely. The images and data on our weather computers became so automated that even an untrained person could put together a reasonable presentation in minutes. A typical weather computer, which handles data and graphics, would cost TV stations tens of thousands of dollars, with additional monthly data fees of several thousand dollars. Email and social media made it easier for people to reach us, but not always for positive reasons.

From a performer standpoint, over my career, I watched as more degreed meteorologists replaced what was traditionally a White male "weatherman." The increased diversity in ethnicity, gender, nationality, and physical appearance has been heartwarming. While public feedback and judgmental comments can be rude, irritating, and insulting, TV is more accepting now of different body shapes, perceived religion, assumed sexual preference, skin colors, and even disabilities. We still have a way to go.

One thing that has not changed is that TV weather broadcasters wear an earpiece, known as an IFB. IFB is an acronym for interruptible foldback, where you normally hear yourself or the program, but the sound can be interrupted by the producer or director to give instructions. That's how we get time cues. Routine cues are short, simple numbers like two, one, thirty, fifteen, ten, and five, where two and one are minutes, and the larger numbers are seconds. Keep in mind, the cues arrive as we are talking, hopefully between our words or sentences, but sometimes during something important that we are saying. We might also be given a cue to stretch, meaning talk longer, especially when there's a technical issue in getting to the next element of the newscast. Toward the end of our segment, we get a wrap cue, meaning finish up your thought or sentence and end. Cut means immediately stop. That's the harsh cue when we've talked far too long and are throwing off the commercial breaks, or when there is breaking news of critical importance. Sometimes the producer or director hits the wrong button, thinking they are talking to an anchor or reporter, when they are talking to the meteorologist in the middle of a segment. Needless to say, that's extremely distracting. It's when you notice the weather anchor yanking their earpiece out. We may also receive time cues by hand signals if there's a studio camera operator. At some stations, time cues are displayed on a monitor.

The other thing that has not changed is the art of communication, which includes how you speak and pronounce words. How do you pronounce coupon, pecan, or salmon? A man was upset with me because I pronounced gibbous with a soft g rather than a hard g, but either one is acceptable. Neither is common! It's not a word that most people use in conversation! Many words and names have regional pronunciations that vary. Car might be pronounced *car* with a hard r in Atlanta, *caw* in New York, and *cah* in Boston. I know people who make it two syllables as *car-uh*! Many words come from other languages. The broadcaster's dilemma is, for example, do you pronounce a French word as it would be spoken in France, or do you use the direct English translation, or do you use the Americanized pronunciation?! The same city name used in different regions can have different local pronunciations. The goal is to speak so that your audience understands, but that requires compromise in the rules of grammar!

I've benefited from the many challenges I've faced in forecasting and trying to be a more effective communicator. I've also personally benefited from meaningful relationships forged with colleagues and competitors. Having lunch or dinner with meteorologists from other TV stations is not unusual. People are always surprised to see us TV weather folks from different stations together in public. Because of what we do, there are few others who can really relate to our work lives.

While there are some TV markets where staff at different TV stations don't get along, or may be antagonistic toward each other, I've been pleased to always have worked in cities where the broadcast meteorologists and National Weather Service, and other weather professionals, have gotten along. To me, the meteorologists at other TV stations are competitors and rivals but not enemies. It's like when you and your childhood best friend go to different high schools. We share the same mission to serve, educate, and protect the public. From a practical standpoint, any of us can go from being a competitor to being a co-worker, so the Golden Rule of treating people the way you want to be treated definitely applies.

Just another weathercast,
written in 1994 but holds true today

9:00 am. I enter the weather office and flick on the lights. Immediately, my eyes sweep across the room for a glance at the weather map and data printers. No paper jams. That's good but the data printer is down to about a half inch of paper. As I replace the paper my sense of hearing kicks in. Silence! That's bad. This time of day I should hear maps churning out of the printer. All I hear is beeps from my graphics computer as it ingests satellite and radar images. Once I finish changing the paper, I step to the map printer to check all cables and connections and reset it just in case ... still nothing. I'll give it a few minutes. In the meantime, I listen to my voice mail: the intern says he can't make it today; a viewer wants the daily temperatures for half of 1989; an observer gives his local readings, and notes that the dewpoint is rising; and my former agent wants to have lunch. "A job offer?" I wonder. Still nothing on the printer so I call the data vendor. The number is long-ago memorized from many days like this. The operator answers and puts me on hold to be serenaded by a country-western version of "Stormy Weather." "They must be having transmission difficulty," I think aloud. All the customers call at once to jam the lines whenever there's a major problem. Two minutes elapse. I maximize time by checking the satellite and radar images in the graphics computer to ensure everything looks ok. Phone cradled between shoulder and head, I type in commands to view images. "Don't know why there's no sun up in the sky…" With a sputter and squeal the map printer springs to life. "Now that's music to my ears," hanging up the phone. Time to sort the dozens of maps sitting in the bin.

9:20 am. All maps sorted. Everything's in order. I go to the newsroom for a preliminary check with the newscast producer. She's munching on doughnuts sent by a sponsor. Payola? I tell her we'll see afternoon thunderstorms—our first in a while. "What time?" she asks, brushing crumbs off her keyboard. "… Can't say yet; I'll get back to you on that." The producer continues, " Ok, here's what we've got. News is slow today so we might lead with weather. Oh, by the way, we may want you to do weather live tonight from on top of Memorial Bridge."

The bridge is narrow, I recall. "Are they closing a lane?" "Oh, no. I meant on top of the bridge tower," she says, with a straight face. "You've got to be kidding! Do you know how small the tower is and how windy it is that high above the river?" I can only think about an old movie I saw in which a depressed circus clown made his way to the top of a bridge tower and was blown off by wind. "No way," I say, "that's not in my contract!" The producer reminds me, "You don't have a contract."

9:30 am. On the way back to the weather office, the mail courier hands me letters and says he thinks I have a guest in the lobby. "Guest, what guest?" I don't remember inviting somebody in. I step swiftly to the reception area and peek through the glass to see two college-aged men looking at the station's awards case. The security guard points to them and waves, signifying that they seem harmless. Some people who come in off the street are not! I enter the lobby and the two spot me. The taller gushes, "Look, I know you're busy but we're huge fans of yours and we were wondering if ..." "If we could have your autograph," the other finishes. I smile, half from appreciation and half from amusement. As I sign their notebooks, the taller starts, "Do you think the ozone thing is real? I mean, I heard on the radio a scientist said ..." I give him a quick answer. "Well, how about global warming?" the other asks. Shaking their hands, I explain that that's a long answer. The taller one begins another question, but I cut him off to remind him that I am busy.

They apologize and turn to leave, pledging to watch me "all the time." As they exit, I overhear one whisper to the other, "He looks taller on TV." Heading back to the weather office, I open my mail to find student letters from a school that I had visited; a realtor trying to sell me a condo; a memo for a meeting that was two days ago; and an invitation from the National Dandruff Society to host their banquet. How that relates to weather, I don't know. Maybe they're trying to tell me something.

9:45 am. In the weather office, I start analysis of weather charts. Using multicolored pencils, I trace and highlight significant features. Climate records let me know if anything unusual has occurred on this date. Precipitation this month has been zero. It's dry.

10:10 am. The phone rings and pulls me out of deep thought. The caller says, "I enjoy your weathercasts but ..." I hold my breath. "... but you seem to always stand in front of the states where my relatives live." I pause. Exhale. Realizing that the caller is sincere, I explain my job is to focus on the local area, but I do add, "I'll see what I can do." Resuming analysis, I start a program in my graphics computer that will redraw satellite images to a custom projection. This is to maintain the station's "look". A pencil falls off the desk and rolls under some equipment. I reach down between two cabinets and see two tiny eyes peering at me. My heart skips half a beat until I realize it's only one of the station's mice. A nuisance, but not exactly dangerous. The mouse scampers away. As I reach for the pencil, I'm careful not to disturb the spaghetti-like connecting cables for our computer systems. The last time I moved a cable, one of the computers crashed.

10:15 am. The phone rings and the caller thinks he has reached the local hospital. Wrong number! I'm called into the studio for a lighting check. We've had problems lately with certain colors becoming transparent in front of the green chroma key wall. The floor crew is moving slowly, and I fidget, thinking about wasted time. As I watch the monitor, the camera brings me into focus. One by one, a computer in the control room removes the colors of the spectrum until there is not much left besides my head and hands. I move as in a mock weathercast, while the floor director snickers. Minutes pass. The camera operator looks out from behind the lens and asks what the weather will be in Hawaii. Everyone hisses out of jealousy. They know he'll be on vacation in a week. "Now does it really matter?" I ask.

10:25 am. Finally, the lighting looks good; I'm finished, but behind schedule. In the weather office, the "message waiting" light is flashing on the phone. A viewer wants to know how to set a barometer. I'll handle that later. I get back to analysis and complete my forecast.

11:00 am. Heading back into the newsroom, I hear reports of an industrial fire crackling on the scanners.

"There's our lead story," I guess. A reporting crew rushes past me, heading to the fire. I tell the producer we can still expect our first thunderstorms in the afternoon. "Great!" she exclaims, with a little too much enthusiasm. "I'll put weather right after the fire at the top of the show. Tease the weather segment at the end of the second block at 12:12 and I'll give you 2 minutes at 12:15." I protest a two-minute weathercast on a day when we get our first active weather in a while. "OK," the producer says, "2:30, but a tight 2:30." This means I'm going to be rushed through the segment. As I turn to walk away, the assignment editor catches me. "You're not gonna wear that tie!?" he says. "We can trade," I quip. He continues, "Not on your life. I thought you said we were gonna get snow; you guys are always wrong." I keep walking. This has become a daily ritual; one I can do without.

11:05 am. After glancing out the window, it's time to start my graphics. I scribble on the nearest map what I plan to create and in what order I'll use the graphics on-air. First, I draw a surface map and then start on a temperature band map. The office lights dim for a split second. I hear a collective groan from the newsroom. We just had a power surge due to construction next door. Half the electronics systems in the station must be rebooted. After rebooting, I lose the map and have to start over. Five wasted minutes.

11:30 am. A few weather observers call in readings. One notes cumulus clouds building rapidly. I check our radar. No rain yet. I pull the latest charts off the map printer and take a quick look before I finalize my forecast. The font operator comes in to pick up my forecast, looks at it and says, "Can't you do any better?" I shake my head. On the way out the door, the font operator collides with the producer. Everybody is rushing as we get closer to air-time. The producer continues past the weather office and yells, "I think I need some time back, that fire is into extra alarms." I shrug and nod my head thinking sarcastically, "What a surprise."

11:45 am. I clip on my wireless microphone and resume creating weather graphics. From this point on, I'm careful of what I say since my mic can be turned on in the control room at any time. More observers call. They're late but on active weather days observer reports are very useful.

11:46 am. I put my lunch on top of a monitor to warm it. The engineers don't like this.

11:49 am. I put on makeup and comb my hair. "Oh well, that's the best I can do."

11:50 am. Microphone check. It's fine.

11:51 am. While checking over my graphics, I almost hit "delete all." Close call! That's a bad feeling to see 45 minutes of work disappear. I debate starting another map vs. doing a little more detailed analysis.

11:53 am. Isolated showers appear on the radar.

11:54 am. The floor crew is sitting casually in the studio while the news writers and editors are frantically finishing late stories.

11:55 am. The news anchor rushes into the studio with scripts trailing behind her. "Five minutes!" the floor director yells.

11:57 am. "Three minutes." I hurriedly complete my graphic and save it.

11:58 am. "Two minutes." The phone rings. "No way," I think, no one should be calling at this time. I let the voice mail take the call.

11:59 am. "One minute." The radar shows stronger showers now. Some may be weak thunderstorms. The floor director counts down, "five, four, three, two ..."

12:00 pm. The anchor starts, "Good afternoon, a major fire is raging ..." Soon a reporter appears live at the scene of the blaze. I look at the background to get a view of the sky condition. The smoke is moving rapidly, letting me know that the winds have picked up. I know I'll be called to the studio any minute, but in the meantime, I retrieve and plot the current conditions. Not a minute to waste now.

12:03 pm. The reporter starts into a closing cadence, so I head to the studio. The floor director waves me off, signaling that I am no longer in the first segment. I go back to finish my graphic.

12:05 pm. As I plot temperatures, I listen to the message left on the phone mail. An observer reports thunder but no rain. I study the radar for 10 seconds and can now see indications of weak thunderstorms. I'll update the forecast. As I pick up the phone to call the font operator, the floor director rushes in, " We need you in 45 seconds!" "Huh? You just told me ..." "It changed," the director snaps back, "get out here now!" I punch a few keys to display the latest radar and move swiftly to my chair on the set.

12:07 pm. The anchor finishes her story and looks at me. "Another nice one?" she asks. Realizing that she has not been outside in four hours, I reply, "Well, not exactly, things are changing." I call for the radar but all I see on the monitor is myself as I ad lib. "Did I punch the wrong key?" I wonder to myself. I call for it again. Bingo. There it is.

The floor director circles her hand in the air letting me know that my time is up. We go to a commercial.

12:08 pm. The data printer in the weather office has a special weather statement with small hail being reported. Now I call the font operator with an update, hoping that in the rush, words will be spelled correctly.

12:11 pm. The news goes back to the fire. Glancing at the screen, I decide to incorporate some meteorological reasoning behind the volatility of the fire in my weather segment.

12:12 pm. All my graphics are done so I put them into a sequence for playback on the air. I can't use all that I created since my time has been reduced to 2 minutes. What a waste!

12:13 pm. The floor director pokes her head into the office, "Call the producer," she says. That's not good. It usually means I'm going to lose more time. The producer asks, "Can you do it in 1:30?" I respond, "Only if I must, there's hail moving in." "OK," she says, "two minutes, but a tight two. No chit chat and I'm dropping your tease." I think of all the preparation I've done for just two minutes of presentation. That's TV news.

12:14 pm. I run though my graphics sequence to see how well it flows. One last minute check of the radar and data shows nothing new. I look out the window.

12:16 pm. Commercial. I head to the studio.

12:18 pm. We're on. The anchor introduces me. I'm in front of the green wall where my maps are electronically simulated. The camera is not framed well, so I feel like I have to duck to stay in the picture. I ad lib a synopsis and go to the updated radar. Meanwhile, a news intern rushes into the studio with scripts and trips over a camera cable. Someone chuckles but I maintain my focus as the floor director gives me a wrap-up cue. Out of the corner of my eyes, I can see that the news anchor is not listening to my forecast, so I tell the viewers that I'll have an update on the evening news and return control of the newscast to the news anchor. No questions. No comment. No time.

12:20 pm. Commercial. Back to the weather office to check on any changes.

12:26 pm. Another power surge, I reboot my graphics computer ... just in case.

12:27 pm. Another commercial. Lots of commercials means the station is making money. By now the anchor is more relaxed. She's shooting baskets with crumpled-up scripts. The floor director is not so relaxed. She runs into the office, "We lost the last live shot, can you fill a minute?" "Oh sure," I think, "now they want me. At least I get to use the graphics that I had to drop." "No problem," I tell her.

12:29 pm. I'm on the set, finally able to have a normal interchange with the news anchor and give the viewers additional, unhurried information.

12:30 pm. We sign off. A commercial. I breathe.

Alan Sealls

CHAPTER 7

My Early Career
Growing up

Not everyone has a career that offers challenge, enjoyment, respect, and a good salary. I was fortunate to find such a career as a television and radio broadcast meteorologist. Broadcast meteorology is a unique profession that allows me to be a scientist, instructor, informer, actor, role-model and somewhat of a "celebrity" and "influencer." I never really wanted a more-common career because I always liked to be different. I wanted a job where my daily routine wouldn't be monotonous. Just about everything that I've accomplished I had planned, once I settled on my path; but sometimes, I look back at the places I've been and the impact I've had and ask myself, "Did I really do that?!"

As a kid, performing was always a strong desire, and I was fascinated by weather. In elementary school, my first career choice was professional trumpeter, but I wasn't that good at playing trumpet! My second choice was professional baseball player, and I also wasn't as good as I thought I was!

I had an interest in weather since about 3rd grade at Holmes school in my hometown of Mount Vernon, NY, when I found out that clouds were made of water, yet they still float! Other things that made me want to become a meteorologist were seeing lightning during a snowstorm, and getting caught in a thunderstorm that produced hail, while I was a kid.

I attended Vernon Heights Congregational Church, and I was a Boy Scout for a short time, until the troop disbanded. I was a paperboy for many years. I played minor league baseball (one step below little league) and spent my free time riding my bike or playing paddleball at Memorial Field. Between walking to elementary school (nearly 1 mile) and my paper route and recreation, I was frequently outside, in a region that had 4 seasons of weather, and sometimes weather extremes.

My dad worked behind the scenes at CBS News in New York. He and my mom religiously followed news in the local newspaper, radio and on TV, so subconsciously, TV and radio weather were always on my mind, but I never purposely watched TV news or weather! I was more interested in weather than in TV news. Growing up, the two local weathercasters I did see the most were Dr. Frank Field, and Mr. G. (Irv Gikofsky). My dad set me up to meet with Mr. G. when I was in high school and that confirmed that TV weather was a field that fit my interest in science, performing, and community service. No one person influenced me to become a meteorologist. It was just the profession that combined all of the things I liked to do. While in high school I finally realized the best job you can have is one where everyone needs what you have — weather information!

I graduated in the top 7% from Mount Vernon High School (MVHS). High school wasn't hard, but I could have done much better if I had tried. My teachers were good and so were my guidance counselors. They kept me on track. My parents made sure of that, too, by being active and visible. I always did my assignments. I later learned ... apply yourself and make sure you learn everything that is being taught. If you have trouble in a certain area, ask for extra help or get tutoring but DON'T GIVE UP. The payoff in the end is worth all the effort. That goes for all endeavors, beyond schooling.

My favorite subject at MVHS was band. I was a pretty decent teen musician, but not trumpeter. My best grade subject was English, followed by math. Classmates laughed in 11th grade when I told them I had decided to pursue broadcast meteorology. They weren't laughing to be mean; they just couldn't envision that as a profession. At later class reunions and encounters, almost everyone said how proud they were of me. That's a nice feeling. My great-grandmother, who was born in 1892, always commented that her father was fairly good at understanding weather and sharing his projections with others. She was certainly proud of me.

My parents raised me to believe that anything is possible, with preparation and persistence. Avoid people who are moving in the wrong direction and do what's right, even when you don't want to! For any positive thing that I tried, they supported me 100%. I tell any student, and even most adults, every opportunity that exists in the world is in front of you and within your grasp. Graduate with good grades. Stay away from drugs. Don't create a child before you are ready and able to support a family. Don't break the law. Treat every human being the way you want to be treated. Read and expand your mind. Never stop learning. You've heard it all before, but it is all basic advice that works. Don't be afraid to leave home and travel. The rest of the world is a lot different from where you live.

College life

I decided to get a Bachelor of Science degree in meteorology from Cornell University. I was accepted there and at several other schools in the Northeast with meteorology programs. I could have majored in broadcasting, journalism, or communications but I wanted a solid foundation in weather. The degree makes me marketable in other meteorology careers such as private forecasting or consulting. While at Cornell, I took the majority of my electives in communications where I was able to tie weather to most of my assignments.

The hardest part about becoming a meteorologist is the calculus and physics. It's often hard to figure out what those things have to do with clouds and rain but once you make the connection, it's easy. I made the mistake of thinking I didn't need to understand everything that I was being taught in college and I ended up having to repeat classes when I went to graduate school.

I learned a lot at Cornell but also had a great social life. Sometimes the social life took priority over the academic life. Outside of class, I was a residence hall advisor. I was also a mobile disc jockey which led to me securing a slot as a Saturday disc jockey at WICB-FM college radio station in my senior year. I learned to ad lib, relate to the audience, read the weather, and most importantly, to be myself on-air. I carefully reviewed each broadcast and worked on overall improvement, especially in enunciation. I also attempted to soften my New York accent since strong regional accents can be a hindrance in professional broadcasting.

Each of my college summers was spent working. I had a lot of temporary jobs, like substitute teaching in my hometown; taking inventory in a furnace parts factory; cleaning up a cafeteria, with duties as a DMO—Dish Machine Operator; and then working as an MHW—

Mental Health Worker—at a small psychiatric facility, where I learned mental health is not outwardly visible, and many people deal with mental health issues. I also learned that you cannot tell who has or doesn't have mental balance issues until you really get to know someone.

The summer before my senior year, I applied for and was selected for an internship at The Weather Channel in Atlanta. This was invaluable for several reasons: I was able to apply knowledge acquired in college while learning the more practical aspects of broadcast meteorology; I made professional contacts and further qualified myself for a career; and I lived in a different part of the country where I experienced different weather patterns as well as a different culture. Working rotating shifts made me realize that weather is 24/7. Up until that point, I figured that when I went to bed, weather stopped!

Following the internship, in my senior year I had the fantastic opportunity to deliver a weekly weathercast at a local cable TV station, for more hands-on experience. Ithaca College's communication department was kind enough to let Cornell meteorology students be a part of their newscasts. My performance was as horrible as that of any other beginner, but I doubt many people were watching. During this time, in 1985, I applied to graduate school. I wasn't sure if after graduation I would want to hit the job market or continue schooling. By the spring of my senior year, I did not have any job offers, so I decided to work toward a master's degree for my own edification and because not many weathercasters have two meteorology degrees. In addition, relatively few African Americans hold higher degrees in the physical sciences and we need to be better represented. Had I gotten a good job offer upon graduation, I doubt that I would have gone on to graduate school. I'm glad now that graduate school was my path.

Graduate school

Florida State University (FSU) offered me financial aid in the form of a teaching assistantship which allowed me to instruct while working toward a master's degree. I strongly believe that one of the most effective ways to learn a subject and learn how to communicate is through teaching that subject to others. The meteorology department at FSU was in the midst of developing a television and radio broadcast area, which was another great opportunity to learn and hone my broadcasting skills. Aside from the on-camera practice, I was able to learn how to use graphics computers and basic video editing equipment. That was before personal computers became so common.

Graduate school was rigorous, and I had serious doubts in my first semester as to whether I would continue. I was alone and not having any fun. A "B" average was required in my program, and I failed to apply myself. At the end of the semester, after nearly failing a course, the dean of the college called me into his office and informed me I would need to turn the grades around in order to remain at the university. His tone of voice implied that he did not think I was capable of doing so. I was offended, and that turned out to be the spark I needed. This was to be the biggest academic challenge I had ever faced. Through the support of my family, professors, and friends, I decided to remain and give it 100%.

I was the only African American in the meteorology department, aside from one professor. At that time, there were literally just a handful of Black meteorology professors in the United States. My classes were in only two different buildings. I rarely was able to walk the campus and interact with other students. I didn't have a car, so I felt isolated. In the off-campus graduate housing where I lived, people were not very social. This is not what I had in mind for sunny Florida. In my first semester, Hurricane Kate struck Tallahassee just before Thanksgiving. Sitting by myself in an apartment with no electricity, listening to the winds howl, it struck me that if you are in the wrong place at the wrong time, you have no control over your future.

Somehow, I took all of these negatives and turned them into positives. I used this time to focus on my program. I became so intense in my efforts that I ended up with straight A's the following semester. I did so well in my calculus and physics courses that other students came to me for help. There was never a doubt that I was capable of excelling but there had never before been a reason to prove it to myself or anyone else.

From thereafter, the highlights of my weeks were teaching my class of undergraduates in weather, and the weathercasting practice in front of a video camera. The meteorology department was flexible enough that I could tailor my coursework toward my objective of being an on-camera meteorologist. Instead of a more traditional research project, my final work was a telephone survey of the public's perception of weathercasts and associated terminology. My research paper was entitled "Clearing up Cloudy Weather Terminology."

As unhappy as I was in my social situation, I successfully completed my master's program in four semesters with no regrets. It was a short period to invest in the knowledge and confidence I gained that remains with me.

While you don't need a master's degree for TV broadcasting, I highly recommend it if you are inclined and able to go after it. The downside is higher education requires money and time. The other potential short-term downside is for some entry-level TV jobs, a person with a master's degree might be perceived as a threat by the rest of the weather staff, since so few broadcasters have one. The long-term benefits override all of the downsides. You become more marketable, especially in larger markets. The master's gives you more knowledge which translates into credibility and confidence. You will be perceived by the public and your peers as being smarter, and you actually may be! You will be qualified as a meteorologist outside of TV. In your middle and late career, you should be paid more than most other folks at your level.

In my final semester at Florida State, I began applying for jobs in small TV markets. TV and radio markets are ranked by the number of viewers or listeners in a given "Area of Dominant Influence" (ADI), which is proportional to the population of a given area. A demo (or resume) videotape accompanied each resume that I sent, as standard practice in the broadcasting industry. I found listings of job openings in the communications trade magazines in the school library. By graduation day, nothing had materialized but I wasn't concerned. I was just happy that it was over, and I knew I could find any job to support me in the meantime.

The day after graduation in 1987, I drove up the east coast to visit friends and family. Along the way, while at my parent's house, I got a call from my advisor, Jon, saying that WALB-TV in Albany, GA (the 151st TV market), was looking for a weathercaster. I was not about to turn around and return to apply for the job. I asked him to get one of my resume tapes from my desk and send it, along with a resume, to the station. I then called the station to express interest in the opening and informed them my materials were "in the mail," then I put it out of my mind and continued my journey.

After returning to Tallahassee a week later, I was called by the station for an interview with the news director, Jerry. Albany is 60 miles from Tallahassee, so I drove. The interview went well, and the station had me go for a physical exam and drug test just in case they decided to hire me. I had extra time in the afternoon, so I drove around the city to get an idea of what it was like. I had decided then that any reasonable offer they might make I would accept. I was ready to work!

Albany, Georgia

A few days later I was called with the job offer and then hired to make my first professional broadcast four weeks after graduation. My salary was set at $14,000 a year. That was half of a typical starting salary for someone with a master's degree. I was a weekend meteorologist and weekday news photographer/videotape editor and occasionally a reporter. While I preferred to be a full-time meteorologist, I saw the benefit of becoming well-rounded in other aspects of broadcasting. I was even given the chance to co-host live programs not related to weather. I enjoyed the city and area and planned to be there about 2 years before I would move on to a better opportunity. I was quickly amazed at the positive response of the public to me simply because I was on television. In my transition from being a student to becoming a professional, it took me a while to get used to being addressed as "Mr. Sealls." Every time I heard that, I thought to myself, "No, I'm Alan. Mr. Sealls is my dad!"

From a historical perspective, it was interesting to note that I was a young Yankee with two college degrees and brown skin in a city where Dr. Martin Luther King Jr. was jailed 25 years earlier for promoting civil rights. I never had a negative experience, although that's probably due to me being in front of the camera. People saw me as the TV weather forecaster rather than a Black guy. My African American co-workers did tell me of their encounters with overt racism in southwest Georgia.

Within 7 months I applied for and earned my American Meteorological Society (AMS) and National Weather Association (NWA) TV weathercaster certifications. These are valuable, as they attest to high standards of communication, knowledge, and professionalism. Approaching my one-year anniversary, I felt I had gone as far as I could go at that station. I was being overworked as a photographer and reporter and underworked as a meteorologist. I had earned a raise to $15,000 per year but that was not significant when my college friends were earning $30,000 and up. It didn't help that the young lady who I was dating dumped me, to pursue career advancement. That stung, but it was the same thing I had done to a woman I dated a couple of years earlier. It helped me see and regret the hurt I caused.

I started my next job search, again willing to go anywhere for opportunity. Through job listings in broadcasting magazines, and networking with friends and contacts, I learned of positions in medium-sized markets. Most on-air people progress from small to medium markets, so I was aiming for the mid-sized markets. However, when I saw a larger market station with an opening, I sent a resume and demo tape anyway, since I had nothing to lose but the cost of the materials.

My response to an ad in Broadcasting Magazine drew a quick response from a station in Milwaukee. Once again, the only interview that I was granted led to me being hired by the news director, Tom. I competed against more than 70 applicants to get the job as a TV and radio meteorologist at WTMJ TV/Radio in Milwaukee, WI. My starting salary was $28,000 per year. It was a huge step to go from the 151st market to the 28th market with only one year of experience. I had no fear—I knew I was ready. It was also a decent salary jump which put me more in line with other college graduates, although still below average.

Milwaukee, Wisconsin

Four days prior to my first anniversary in Albany, GA, I was on the road in my Datsun 510, with a few foldout roadmaps, a couple of hundred dollars, and all my possessions to a new job in Milwaukee. I was so eager to move on that I didn't stop and realize that if I had stayed 4 more days in Albany, to reach one full year, I would have been paid for one week of vacation.

I was excited about the opportunity and pleased that someone had recognized my talent and ability without me using a TV agent. A few agents did approach me while I was in Albany, but I felt at that time that I could do well by myself. I didn't like the idea of paying someone to do something for me that I could do myself. To make matters worse, one of the agents who had contacted me misrepresented himself as a friend of a friend. I called my friend, Janice, to ask her about the agent and she said that she had only met him briefly.

Upon arriving in Milwaukee in June of 1988, I knew no one there and very little about the city, yet I quickly developed strong friendships and became a part of the community. In fact, that is where I met and married my wife. As a TV and radio weathercaster, I made numerous public appearances on behalf of my station and received a handful of awards. I grew as a meteorologist, broadcaster, and person. I joined several professional associations and attended meetings and conferences whenever possible.

In my job routine, there were dangerous weather situations where I received praise from the public for my calm yet informative handling of the events. In public, I also had very positive feedback. One of the most rewarding experiences was, after having made a school presentation in a town outside of Milwaukee where no Black people lived, receiving a letter from a White 3rd grader stating, "I think Black people are cool." I was probably the first living, breathing Black person this kid had met. I wonder where he is today and what his life perspective became.

Another heartwarming experience I had was when I volunteered to be a "celebrity" bagger at a grocery store, to raise money for a charity. There was one man whose food I bagged before he began to walk away. He took a few steps, turned around, reached into his wallet, and said, "If Alan Sealls could come here on a Saturday to bag groceries, I can make a donation." That is a plus of being on TV. You can influence people to do positive things.

Milwaukee was a clean, comfortable city for a young professional. I again found myself in situations where I was the only Black person at a golf outing, or a fundraiser, or in doing things that Blacks native to that city had not done. I was seen as the TV meteorologist until the day I received my first overt racist comment. It was only a matter of time. On a day when I was filling in for the main weathercaster, right after the weather segment a viewer called and was put through to the weather office. I answered the phone.

"Why do you have that person on TV?" he demanded to know. I wasn't sure if it was a prank call, so I answered, "Excuse me?" The caller continued, "I came up from Alabama 20 years ago to get away from those chocolate niggers." I was caught off guard but forced myself to respond politely for the man to call my supervisor the next day if he had a problem with any of our on-air presentation. I had to go out and finish the newscast with a forced smile and a sick feeling in the pit of my stomach.

What's ironic is that the caller did not even know it was me he was talking to but that's part of the senselessness of racism. I came to find that the station received similar calls whenever we had two Black anchors filling in for a newscast normally anchored by Whites. The racism never surprises but always disappoints me. What's also ironic, is that two decades later, I would end up being the first Black TV meteorologist in Mobile, Alabama, just as I was the first in Milwaukee, Wisconsin, and in Albany, Georgia.

In my mid-20s, in Milwaukee, I definitely saw how people treated me differently, in a celebrity sort of way, because I was on TV. Those who know me will tell you that I'm a down-to-earth guy who tries hard to be fair and honest and have fun! People who meet me and don't know what I do for a living would never guess, because for as much as I enjoy my profession, when I'm not at work I'm the same kid who grew up in Mount Vernon—just older and wiser. TV doesn't make me who I am. It's just part of my job. Life in front of a TV camera has the downside of dealing with people who only see you as a TV personality, not a human being, and dealing with people who want to take advantage of your kindness, and your perceived dollar resources.

While in Milwaukee, I took advantage of all opportunities to improve and build a stronger resume. My regular TV and radio shift was weekend weather and then midday weather three days a week. I filled in for the morning meteorologist and chief meteorologist frequently. Even though I'm not a morning person, I had no problem getting up early to be on the morning newscasts. It was exposure to a different audience, with repetition to sharpen my skills. There was a stretch where the other two meteorologists had back-to-back vacations, resulting in me working 17 days in a row. That was perfectly fine with me.

In the middle of my contract, I gradually sent out over 130 inquiries or applications to all TV stations in the top 30 markets. My goal was to have my work seen, to set me up for later opportunities. Remember, this was before social media! Each letter was mailed with a broadcast-standard ¾" videotape. Some tapes were those that were discarded by my station, while others I had purchased as recycled for a few dollars each. Combine that with the $2.90 cost of mailing them, and the cost of packaging, and that easily exceeded a total of $5 for each mailing. I saved money by mailing in waves. I would send tapes to all the top five markets, for example. From the multiple rejections, some would send my tapes back and I would reuse them for the next round of applications, in markets 6 through 10. I cued each tape to exactly 3 seconds before the video started so that if the tape came back to me, I could tell how much, if any, the news director watched! I used a spreadsheet to keep up with and track this valuable information. The spreadsheet included when managers left stations, leading to potential opportunities for me at their old station or their new station.

From my careful notetaking, I found that from nearly 130 videotapes I sent to TV stations, one third of the stations never responded. Of the two thirds that did respond, the reply was almost always "no." A handful had words of encouragement or constructive criticism. Several news directors responded with a note for me to follow-up at some later point. Two responses did lead to interviews. A third of the TV stations did not return my videotape. That was customary practice because of the significant mailing expense. It took one station a full year to return my tape. Another station returned my tape 16 months later! One station even returned someone else's tape to me, but at least they tried!

At the end of my 3-year contract, in 1991, I received a substantial raise to $40,000, and a short contract extension, finally putting me where I would have been 4 years earlier if I had gone into other sectors of meteorology. I had also been receiving job offers from other stations. The man who hired me in Milwaukee left the business and his replacement "offered" me a reduced salary. He offered "thirty-six." I asked in all seriousness if that was thirty-six hundred dollars per month. It wasn't. He was offering $36,000 per year. I couldn't accept that. I wanted a raise, and he wanted to cut my pay. I might have accepted no raise but even settling at a midpoint was not good enough for me. A pay cut, after 4 years of strong contribution to a team of meteorologists, where each had a master's degree, was not an option, just based on principle.

Because I had no other job prospects, my toughest professional decision to that point was to not sign the new contract offer, but it wasn't really difficult. I was recently married, but my wife supported that decision. I really liked Milwaukee and my friends, co-workers, and extended family. As luck and timing would have it, one of the tapes that I had sent out landed on a news director's desk just as he was searching for a weekend weathercaster. The news director in Chicago, the 3rd largest market, Paul, called me shortly after my announced "resignation" in Milwaukee and within weeks hired me at Chicago superstation WGN-TV, in 1992.

CHAPTER 8

My Middle Career
Chicago, Illinois

Chicago is a major TV market. TV salaries are proportional to the population of a market, so I worked less and made more money than I did in Milwaukee. Even with a higher cost of living in Chicago, I came out ahead, financially and professionally. Part of the reason for that was Chicago was a union market, where much of TV station staff was a member of either an engineering union, or a "talent" union. For those of us in front of the camera, the union was the same one that television and Hollywood actors were a part of. That took an adjustment, because I had never worked as a union member before, so I could only envision striking union workers on a cold winter day huddled around a barrel of burning wood, trying to stay warm. It wasn't like that!

Unions provide support for workers, often with healthcare and investment options and pensions. They advocate for fair compensation and a safe and supportive workplace. I later became involved as an observer with union activities and contract negotiations and saw how valuable all of this was.

The move was excellent in all respects. I was seen nationally on a superstation. I was given the opportunity to do reporting on science features. The station supported my community outreach efforts by reimbursing me for mileage to speaking engagements. The news department paid for one professional development conference per year. I was being groomed to move up into a full-time position. I was building a strong following just as I had done in Milwaukee. My wife and I bought a house. Then the wind shifted. The news director who hired me in Chicago was let go and I started a lesson in Job Politics 101.

The news director's replacement was a lady who had never been news director before. Her people skills were horrible. She was inconsistent, disingenuous, and played favorites. She changed rules and policies verbally and instantly, when they suited her agenda. Twice, I was passed over for a promotion. By itself, that was not a problem. The problem was how it occurred, with me either being left in the dark, or not given the full story of what was available and why I wasn't given the opportunity. TV news is very subjective, to the point that my credentials didn't carry as much weight as the opinion of a hiring manager who thinks you are the right person in appearance, voice, gender, ethnicity, height, weight, and background, to get people to watch.

Once by the news director, and once by one of her middle managers, I was set up to fail or create conflict in the weather office. It was not obvious to me at the time. One incident that was very obvious is when I was not paid for an assignment. I requested to be paid, and the news director balked. I ended up having to file a grievance with my union to have it resolved. I was eventually paid. In each of these incidents, I stood up to her, and that further and unfairly limited any opportunity of advancement. When she started as news director, she told me, "You have a good future here." Months later, she turned cold and told me, "You could stay, or you could leave"! She even cut my workload and salary by more than 50%. I decided to stay until something better came along. I outlasted her. Our corporate owner saw that her style and weaknesses made her a liability. They let her go, after another employee literally threatened to harm her.

I no longer had a contract at WGN after having had one for my first two years there. I also worked much less than I'd ever worked before. Neither of these was my choice. Given the negatives, I still loved what I did as a weathercaster. With more free time than I wanted, I returned to academia at Columbia College as a part-time meteorology instructor, simply because a colleague asked me if I was willing. I did not realize until years later that teaching is a natural part of my personality, and it's certainly what all weather broadcasters do on a daily basis.

I also wrote a monthly weather column for a local community newspaper. I was able to host the weather segment of an outside educational program because a viewer who was an independent producer involved with the project thought I'd do a good job at it. Similarly, a colleague referred a person to me who needed a meteorologist for two educational weather videos, distributed by a local company called United Learning. All of these projects and endeavors had teaching as a foundation. I got to attend all of my professional conferences and seminars, so I kept busy, expanding my knowledge base, while also continuing weekly appearances in schools and throughout the community.

After being exposed to the world of educational videos via United Learning, one particularly rewarding endeavor I undertook was to write, produce, shoot, edit and host my own video for kids on severe weather safety. High-quality video cameras had come down in price, at the same time that my wife started her own video production business. That allowed me to do everything myself. I enjoyed being in control of a project that had meaning. Furthermore, the video was significant in that I created a quality piece of work, distributed nationwide, without any help or resources from my employer. The video increased my exposure as a meteorologist, while providing another source of income.

The educational videos for kids blossomed when United Learning was bought by Discovery Education. I continued to produce more and more videos over the decades that followed, that were later also distributed by another international company, named Boclips. One of my best friends from childhood called me one day, excited that his son's homework had my name on it, from one of the lesson plans I had created. It was a great feeling to create something valuable and healthy and educational and be paid for it! I have about 100 videos that I've produced, that continue to be used domestically and internationally.

At that same time, in Chicago, I stumbled upon the arena of safety videos for businesses. In the middle 1990s, companies were paying several hundred dollars for training videos that either helped them meet Federal safety standards, or that just were beneficial to employees and to company profit. I produced a weather safety video that I marketed and sold for a few years, first as VHS, then as a DVD. It took a lot of effort to sell it, and I only broke even. Similar videos on YouTube and other platforms made it more difficult to make a profit.

I also had another venture of selling a compilation of my weather photos and videos to TV stations, video production houses, and filmmakers. That also was an arduous and expensive project, on which I lost money, and then gave up as more and more weather videos and images were becoming accessible online. I never really considered myself an entrepreneur, but I was. I was able to learn a lot from those failures about marketing, promotions, artwork, databases, mailings, and packaging. I did everything myself. Those are some of the same skills that many media professionals use to advance their careers, in some form or another.

One thing that I'm pretty sure has helped me in my career has been regularly going back to the basics of meteorology and refreshing my knowledge base. Every other year I would reread my introduction to meteorology textbook. I bought a copy of the *Glossary of Meteorology* by the American Meteorological Society. That's a book that lists all words, phrases, tools, and processes related to meteorology.

A positive response from the community is what kept me going. One particularly rewarding incident in Chicago stands out, where I had spoken to a group of students in a summer program about weather. The question, "How much money do you make?" always comes up, so I answered as I usually do, by telling the kids how much money they can make with different scenarios. I showed the kids my bank card and credit cards and explained how they work, saying they must earn them. Then I showed them my library card and told them that's the way to learn and earn. A few weeks later one of the teachers wrote to me and said that several of the students had gone out and gotten library cards. Wherever possible I've always used my influence from being on TV to generate positivity.

Another awesome moment was when I was walking down the street one afternoon. A cab driver passing by noticed me, stopped his cab in the middle of the road, got out, and ran over to me with a broad smile. He vigorously shook my hand and exclaimed, "You look just like me!" He sounded and appeared to be African. My presence on TV gave him a lift. That's the way I feel when I see other African Americans achieving in positions where we have traditionally been left out.

It's always funny when I meet people who don't watch my station and have a normal interaction with them. Once they find out that I'm on TV they treat me much better, as though I'm different from everyone else. Suddenly, merchants want to give me discounts and show me their finest wares. Others want to introduce me to all their friends and invite me to their homes and communities. All of that is for the wrong reason.

People who have seen me on TV and then meet me in person almost always comment that they expected me to be taller and heavier. Is that a compliment? I am slim, some people would say skinny, and the lights and cameras do distort the picture a little, but people think that in order to be on TV there must be more substance to you than to the average person. TV lighting does change your appearance because the studio lights are angled to highlight your face, whereas in most buildings, the lights hit you from straight overhead. TV broadcasting is an interesting career, but it is also a job like any other.

One of the biggest funny shocks I had, when at WGN, happened after I got home from working my shift. On weekend mornings, I would get up at 3 am and be at work by 4:30 am. Our morning newscast was always replayed on a cable station, after the live broadcast. I lived close enough to the station that I was home before the replay ended. One morning after I had gotten home, and was unwinding, preparing to take a nap, my wife must have been watching the replay, when I heard the announcer say, "Coming up next is Alan Sealls with the weather." I froze and for a split second panicked, until I realized it was a recording! That's a bad feeling not to be in place when your segment starts.

For most of the early part of my career, I had an infrequent, yet periodic, nightmare that something would prevent me from getting to work or being in front of the camera. Other broadcasters say they've had that too. I'm happy to say that that has never happened. There was one close call when I worked in Milwaukee and had stepped out for lunch. Just as I was returning and entering the station parking lot, listening to our radio station at 1 pm, I heard the announcer say, "Alan Sealls will be up with the forecast at 1:04." I rushed into the gated lot, found a spot, ran into the building, and sprinted down the hallway. I made it, with only seconds to spare! But I could barely talk. I couldn't catch my breath. That was a key lesson in that you cannot rush to get in place and expect to speak normally, or even speak at all.

While I've made small mistakes on live TV, I can happily say that I've never done or said anything embarrassing. The closest I came to that was on a live broadcast at a parade. I was randomly picking people out of the crowd to interview. One person I chose, I asked, "What's your name, young lady?" She said, "I'm a boy." Oops! I could only apologize and smile and keep on going with the interview. He had long hair. I probably was not as embarrassed as the young man was. I wonder if he cut his hair after that!

I make it a rule to be on my best behavior when I'm wearing a microphone or when a camera is pointing toward me, even if we are not broadcasting. I act as though there are Girl Scout Brownies and a group of nuns standing by.

Chicago shift

In 1997, I was offered a full-time position as weather producer at the NBC TV station in Chicago. I would be the 4th person on the weather team, mostly off-camera, but sometimes on-camera. I was not very interested, and I made it clear to the general manager that I wouldn't want to stay in a slot like that. Lyle, the general manager, understood and made me a generous offer worth accepting. At the time, the station was in between news directors.

A few months later, a news director was hired, and he brought his team and started hiring staff. Any new manager creates nervousness among employees about the uncertainty of job positions and duties. I was not worried because I never intended to stay long anyway. I had a one-year contract. I was quickly disappointed that my on-air time was cut by the new news director. He redefined the terms under which I was hired. Here again, I saw the politics of a corporate-owned TV station, where it seemed more important to know somebody, than to know something. It was about loyalty or obedience and protecting your position. This was the start of a downhill slide for me, and for the station in another matter.

A few months later, the weather team heard rumors of another weathercaster being hired. We asked the news director, and he said the rumors were not true. Weeks later, that weathercaster walked into the newsroom on a day when the news director was off. Obviously, she was hired. Her role in evenings took away from the main weather anchor's duties and visibility and that created tremendous friction. She was part of the new management team and had 100% support of the news director. I'm sure he thought she could increase ratings, but it seems she was also planted in the weather office to create dissension. Her hiring did not increase ratings. Nobody trusted her, as hard as she tried to form alliances.

The station also tried to hire talk show host Jerry Springer, to do commentary on the 10 pm news. That was a disaster too. Many of the staff, including myself, signed a petition requesting that this not happen. The main anchors resigned. Managers were fired, and yet another management team entered. The new management team followed the cycle of replacing staff. I was coming up to the end of my one-year contract and I was ready to go. I didn't want to work in a place that operated like that. In addition, I never had gotten any real opportunity for advancement, as the 5th member on the weather team, although I objectively had the most professional qualifications as a meteorologist.

In the midst of this, I signed with an agent, referred to me years earlier by the man who originally hired me in Chicago. I saw the value in having a buffer between me and management, along with someone who would always be looking out for my best interest. I did not plan to be caught without a job at the end of my contract.

My first talk with the new news director was positive. I was told clearly that I was not good enough in her judgment to be a prime player. She was straightforward, and that is always helpful. I respected it, although I knew she was wrong! In the following weeks, two of the other weathercasters were offered demotions. One declined and soon left the station.

When I sat down again with the news director, I was told that another weathercaster was hired for our new morning show and, because the weather office would be crowded with 6, I should leave within a couple of months. I was praised for all the work I had done but told in a long-winded way that I was not staying. I asked my manager why it is that companies are so quick to go outside to get another person rather than investing in what is already there. I got another long answer that wasn't really an answer.

You're fired, again

Many of my co-workers were amazed that I was not offered any opportunity to stay with the station, but in the game of politics that's usual. I was the old team, and I'd be a perceived threat to any new players. In your career, plan on being fired, but hopefully not for failing at your duties. If you do nothing wrong, you won't be told "You're fired," but you will hear things like, "We are not renewing your contract," or "Your position is being eliminated," or "We're going in a different direction." Don't take it personally. It will be a shock that knocks you off balance and may be a short-term setback. Take it as an opportunity to find a better overall position.

One week after being let go, I was watching The Weather Channel and their coverage of Hurricane Bonnie. I thought to myself, "I wish I were on-air for this one." The next day the phone rings. It's Craig, a general manager from a cable TV station in Orlando. This is a man who was news director at a sister station when I worked at WGN. I had met him and kept in touch, and recently let him know that I was out of work.

"What are you doing this week?" Craig asked. I replied, "Job hunting." "How'd you like to come down to Orlando and help us out for a few days?"

The next day I was on a plane to Orlando with 4 suits in my bag. I was familiar with the computer system at Craig's station as it was the same one I had just used in Chicago. The next 5 days I was on the air.

Timing! Both Craig and I knew his station couldn't afford to hire me, but we were both in need and the temporary fee was right. The station had not yet finished hiring their weather staff.

A couple of weeks after that, Cindy, my former weather colleague at WMAQ, called from her new chief meteorologist position in Saint Louis. She ended up having her station hire me for 4 days as a weather computer consultant. They had the same weather computer, but it had not been maintained since installation and it needed cleaning up and a few upgrades.

I returned to Orlando for another week of fill-in. One evening, as my shift was ending, one of the reporters handed me a note with a phone number on it and said, "Your brother Harold called." The number was local, but all my brothers lived over a thousand miles away. I was perplexed, but I called. Sure enough, it was my brother who was visiting Orlando! Neither of us knew that the other was going to be there.

Over the course of the next few months, I applied for and received unemployment insurance. It had been suggested to me by my tax planner. I had never considered applying because of a stigma associated with it, and because I had never been unemployed before. I thought I would need it for a brief time. Wrong. I was out of work for almost a year. There should be no stigma in losing a job in which you did your best. Unemployment insurance exists for exactly that reason. I contributed many years to the unemployment fund and deserved the payments.

My wife and I have always been savers, and she was working full-time. Between that and the bi-weekly unemployment checks, we didn't have to change our lifestyle too much. She continued to run her startup video production business while I continued to produce independent weather videos, attend conferences, job hunt, and serve as president of the Chicago Chapter of the AMS—the first Black person, to my knowledge, in a 60-year history. I had plenty of time to do whatever I wanted, but what I really wanted was a full-time weather job with respect and opportunity.

My agent, Rick, stayed busy seeking spots for me. I waited.

Heading south

By late summer of 1999, my unemployment was running out. In August, my agent called with a job opening for a chief meteorologist in Mobile, Alabama, the 62nd market. I had never considered living there and knew nothing about the city. I did the usual research and found that Mobile was the second largest city in Alabama, with warm but changing weather, daily thunderstorms, occasional tornadoes and hurricanes, a lower cost of living, and a large Black population. Data from my annual AMS salary survey projected a lower but decent pay range.

I called the news director to see what he was offering. The position was chief meteorologist. He offered to fly me down. I accepted, although I was ambivalent. He had already seen my resume tape and knew of my work, so I had him send me a VHS tape of his newscasts so that I could gauge the quality of the station.

Shortly thereafter, I landed at Mobile's airport. First thought: "A lot of trailer homes around here." Second thought: "Not bad, compared to Birmingham." Birmingham's airport was stuck in the 1970s.

The news director, Dan, greeted me, and we headed out to his car. It was an old Honda stick shift with manual windows and a rough ride. Dan cranked up the air conditioner to fight off the 90-degree heat. "My wife has the other car." I tried to stay relaxed to avoid sweating as the temperature slowly cooled. Dan drove me east into Mobile from the airport along Mobile's busiest street. Third thought: "This is OK." From what I was seeing, Mobile was like most cities in the United States, with the range of homes, stores, malls, and people.

Upon arrival at the TV station, I went through the routine of meeting everyone. The people seemed nice and welcoming. Having been in the South before, I was not thrown off by some of the regional accents, and how some of the native folks went out of their way to allay any concerns that Southerners are slow and backward.

The physical things that impressed me were that the building was designed as a TV station, the equipment was current and better than that in many large markets, and the main weather computer was the same as what I used in Chicago. A Doppler radar had been ordered and was set to be installed the following month, making WKRG-TV the first in the market to have their own radar. The station also had a leased helicopter.

Most of the managers were overly accommodating and each tried to sell me on the station. The general manager was in place less than 18 months, and the news director less than 6. I saw this as a good sign that I would have at least a few years of stability and security, given that the average tenure of a news director was just a few years. The prior management team had not changed in 20 years! Both the general manager and news director indicated a major commitment to weather and weather equipment. I was satisfied although I had not yet heard any dollar figures. I didn't want to deal with money and have to face these two men every day, so I left that up to my agent.

After a following week of phone calls and emails, the offer was sent to my agent. Neither of us was excited about it but it was sufficient. The contract was for 3 years with an option for me to end my contract after 2 years if I got a job offer in a large market. That's known as an out-clause. I had no other offer for a chief meteorologist position in the prior one-year period. I was probably becoming less marketable, and finances were just getting to the point where I needed to return to full-time work. I couldn't wait indefinitely. I signed the contract. I started the next month, and my wife followed 6 months later, after she closed up her business, settled paperwork, and sold the house.

The job went very well. My reputation preceded me from having been on WGN on cable and satellite. The public reception was warm and overwhelmingly positive. The weather staff supported me and appreciated my skills. I finally was in the type of position that I should have been in 6 years earlier.

As with all of my career moves, I was careful to never talk about how things were done at my previous jobs. That would have been like telling your boyfriend how good your previous boyfriend was. I've also never been one to talk about any of my achievements, education, or background that might make others (unnecessarily) feel less about themselves.

People who don't travel much have preconceptions of what I am or what I should be. They are not all positive. Shortly after starting at WKRG, I got a funny email:

Alan: I am impressed! Am retired professor of sociology, white, old. from Wyoming and living in Pensacola. You are attractive, skilled, personable, and blessed with communication skills. May I write WGN Chicago and ask that they look into considering you for their staff? How else may I help. You are fit for a much larger market. Most sincerely, Lamar.

I never figured out if the man was trying to be funny or if he didn't know that I had already worked at WGN! Either way, it was one of many positive comments I received from White viewers, and from Black viewers. It continues to this day, from random email or messages, and from seeing people when I am out and about.

When I'm out in public, and not working, I try to blend in and not be noticed. I wear earth tones and solid colors with no logos on my clothing. I don't wear any jewelry or anything shiny that could catch someone's eye. At one festival, a man called out my name. I said, "Yes?" He came over and gave me a big hug and said how much of a fan of me he was. He called his wife over, and she looked a little embarrassed. I thanked him for watching and shook his hand, trying to not cause a scene. I shook his wife's hand too. Maybe he had had a few drinks, but he then looked a little embarrassed too. I was flattered but didn't have time to tell him that he shouldn't be embarrassed. This was a young White man.

Two weeks later, I'm in an office store in my work "uniform" and two older White men call out my name. One starts with something I hear often, "What's the weather?!" I chuckled and gave him an answer. Each of them shook my hand but one of them went on to say,

"You're Black, and it doesn't matter!" I said, "I agree!" He grabbed me and gave me a big hug. I was caught a little off guard. He then continued to tell me that he was 83 and had served in the Army with Black people who he saw as just people, not Black people. His friend looked a little embarrassed, but I was amused, and I was appreciative of his action and his sentiment.

I've always been pleased that people recognize the significance of a college-educated Black meteorologist on TV.

In Mobile, I received a call from an elderly woman:

"I'm 69 years old and I have 5 children, all of them married although some are now divorced. And I'm from Mobile. I just want to tell you, when you first started here, I was upset. I said, 'Why couldn't they have hired a nice young White fellow?' I switched stations and tried the rest, but I just wasn't happy with them. So, I turned back and watched again."

The woman went on to say that she had come to appreciate my style and presentation and that I spoke so clearly. She capped off the call by saying that she would be willing to adopt me and accept me into her family! She was serious.

Shortly after I arrived in Mobile, at Robbins Elementary School, in the majority Black community of

Prichard, AL, I went to talk to a 4th grade class. One Black girl looked at me and said aloud, "I thought you were White." She seemed a little embarrassed after her exclamation, but I reassured her that many people assume I'm White before meeting me because they've never seen a Black meteorologist before.

This was only a month after attending the 25th anniversary conference of the National Weather Association (NWA). Held in Gaithersburg, Maryland, it was the largest meeting of the organization. By day two of the conference, when I stepped up to the podium as a session chair, I looked out into the audience and paused, realizing that I was the only professional Black male meteorologist there. Aside from a half-dozen Black students from Jackson State University, there was only one Black woman meteorologist. Neither I, nor anyone else there, could have guessed that 16 years later I would be elected as the first Black president of NWA. For any career advancement, it is critically important to not just be a member of organizations, but to contribute through committees and to accept or seek leadership roles. My involvement in professional societies and groups has paid huge dividends in contacts, opportunity, and visibility.

On my return flight from the conference, I noticed one of the first-class passengers was CNN commentator Wolf Blitzer. I thought to myself, "I guess he commutes from Atlanta to DC to do his program." Six weeks later my agent calls me and asks if I'm interested in filling in on CNN on weekends. Easy answer: Yes! Surprisingly, my new station allowed me to do it. They probably saw it as a good opportunity to show that Mobile's newest chief meteorologist was good enough to be on a national network. While being on local in Mobile Monday through Friday and then appearing on CNN on Saturday and Sunday may have confused people, it also showed them my caliber and abilities.

My first fill-in day at CNN went well except for one thing: I didn't get to be in front of the camera. It turned out to be one of the biggest news days of the year on November 26, 2000, when the decision to the George Bush/Al Gore presidential elections recount from Florida was announced. After much anticipation and excitement from my parents and brothers, it turned out that they could only hear a recorded audio weather segment on CNN's Headline News.

My second opportunity at CNN was a hit. However, it was after a week of working my Monday-Friday normal shift plus the shift of my co-worker. My niece had just visited the week before, and then my nephews were with me from Boston. I was tired all week. I rose on Saturday at 4:20 am, with only 4 hours of sleep, drove 60 miles to Pensacola, Florida, for a one-hour flight to Atlanta. From Hartsfield International, I took a cab to the CNN center and went straight to the weather office. Less than 90 minutes later I was on the air, talking about a major snowstorm in the Northeast. All of my on-air performance was solid, but behind the scenes I could barely focus from being so tired. The day was mentally busy for me, and it was not until I checked into the hotel and sat down that I realized that I was on CNN. I was pleased that I did as well as I did, being so tired. I was also happy that my family got a chance to see me and that they were all excited.

The weather office at CNN was typical of a TV station. It was separated from the newsroom, and it had no windows. I was essentially in a room by myself for the day doing live weather segments, using two different weather graphics computers. One of them I was intimately familiar with, the other I was barely proficient on. I focused on the system that I knew better! Steve, the weather office coordinator and managing producer, was impressed. I laughed on my last day when one of the on-air weather folks remarked how I might want to apply for a job as a weather producer. It was funny because her training and experience wasn't as extensive as mine. It was as though she were saying, "You'd do well here as long as you don't threaten my job security."

Mobile turned out to be the right place for me. For the first time, I was allowed to do weather the way I thought it should be done. That's after people got used to seeing a Black weather guy on TV wearing a double-breasted suit.

In one of my first evaluations, the news director told me that people thought I was overdressed. That was their impression since they were used to seeing male anchors just wearing sportscoats. I had stopped wearing sports coats many years ago because I think suits are more professional and give credibility. My work attire is a uniform, and I've always tried to keep it classy but not obnoxious. It took me years to understand the difference between a good suit and an average suit, and even more years to grasp that certain colors work better with my dark skin tone. These are not things that men are taught when we are young! From shirt to tie to suit and pocket square, everything has to be cohesive in style, fit, color, pattern, and fabric type. One of the challenges for any newscaster is not dressing to the degree that the clothing becomes a distraction, whether it's a really attractive outfit, or an outfit that looks terrible, or one that is just not appropriate for the often serious and formal setting. The clothing is not supposed to overpower the information you are imparting.

In Mobile, I also returned to academia, at the University of South Alabama, where I taught a weather broadcasting course every spring (and I still do). Teaching is a natural hobby that gives me a lot of enjoyment and satisfaction. The course typically had half a dozen students. Most were meteorology majors, but only a couple were really targeting broadcasting as a profession. From each year I taught, one or two students would go on to become professional weathercasters. For those that went into other sectors, the communication and presentation skills I taught were still relevant. It is an awesome feeling to see someone you helped in some small way grow and achieve positive things. Some of my former students went on to work in Mobile as competitors, and one even as a co-worker.

The downside of Mobile was the pace of progress was slow, in the station and in the community. People tended to stick to what they learned earlier in life and not try new things. On the job, I constantly had to catch myself and slow down. For example, a manager would say that we would do a new project. I'd come in the next day ready to go, or halfway done while no one else even gave it a second thought. It was always funny when someone would ask me to do something, and I would have it completed within an hour or a day when they weren't expecting it until the next week. So many news department upgrades to computers or other systems often happened anywhere from months to years after they were scheduled. I often had to piece together two computers in order to get a job done that should have only required one. It was more work for me, which few people realized or cared about, but it made me stronger and more marketable.

In the midst of a station graphics change, I overhauled the weather graphics and standardized them. Using the same standards in the top ten markets and the networks, I tried to impress upon the weather staff that we had equivalent computers and there was no reason our product should look small. Over time they came to appreciate it. After returning from a vacation, I actually had a caller question my whereabouts. She said that not only did I present the weather clearly, but I had the best-looking graphics. That's a compliment. Oftentimes viewers don't even watch the weather until the extended forecast pops up.

Promotions was sometimes a problem area. My station was heavy on promotions to the point that at times it was more important to promote that we did something than actually doing that thing to the best of our ability for a sound journalistic purpose. I had several issues with promotions claiming things about our weather coverage that were not accurate or could not be verified. I never wanted to be called out by the public for saying something that I can't back up.

At WKRG, my agent handled all of the numbers and negotiations in my multiple contracts. That is something I never want to do again. It's not my strength and I don't like haggling. I also don't want to face someone everyday who I felt was unfair or dishonest in negotiations. Of course, many managers try to avoid agents, since it makes their negotiations harder. While my initial salary was low, the regular raises that my agent negotiated quickly put it where it needed to be, over time.

After many years on TV in Mobile, I became a fixture. It just happened through persistence and hard work of trying to be the best I could be, while being there in the worst storms. I had proven my dedication through several severe weather events, visited dozens of schools and civic organizations, and won several local and state awards. I worked with different meteorologists and weather interns, who I hope I helped be the best they could be.

I always tried to be not just a team leader, but a team player, putting in 100%. That meant being available in a weather crisis or staff shortage, as when the rest of my team was sick or out of town and I worked morning, midday, and evening shifts for two and a half days. It meant cancelling personal travel and cutting a trip short to return to work. It regularly meant being the last person to leave the station at night. It meant driving 90 minutes each way to visit a rural school for an hour, before going to work. I could do all of this because I love what I do and have an understanding spouse.

Professionally, that is what we want; but the price you pay, especially in a smaller market, is a loss of privacy. To this day, I forget that when I'm out shopping, that I'm not just me, I'm the weather guy. I do get a kick out of kids being excited to recognize me and see me in street clothes.

Alan Sealls

On the other hand, the adults often slow me down by telling me stories of other TV people they've met or by asking questions. It's always funny to watch people react when they see me in public, but they can't place where they know me from. It starts with them cocking their heads, squinting their eyes, and having a quizzical look. Their expression then breaks out into a broad grin if I talk, and they hear my voice. Other times, people will ask me if they know me from high school or church. Sometimes, I pretend to have no idea why they are asking, just for fun. Other times, I just say the name of my TV station, and then they laugh.

I speak to thousands of kids each year and meet hundreds of adults each year at events and random locations. Increasingly, I recognize people from past events. However, the worst thing some people do is walk up to me and ask, "Do you remember me?" If I didn't have a meaningful interaction with that person, the odds are that I don't remember them. For that reason, when I meet people, instead of saying, "Nice to meet you," I say, "Good to see you"!

In my nearly 20 years at WKRG, each year I got enjoyment from the dozens of community appearances I made. I was invited back to speak at one Baptist church school in Mobile. The kids were excited to see me again and made me feel welcome. We met in the church sanctuary which had a good video projection system. I've spoken at other churches, and I still just don't feel right speaking in the pulpit, so I stayed on the floor, just in front of it!

As always, I spoke about the skills required for my job and the science of meteorology. I'm always careful not to offend or contradict any religious views of science and the history of Earth and humanity. I think I did a pretty good job. One kid asked about other jobs I've had in life, and I was quick to tell them I'd done everything from washing dishes to working in a psychiatric hospital while on break from college. They laughed when I told them I learned that you can't always tell the staff from the patients in those facilities, but I used that opportunity to talk about mental illness and how it's something many "normal" people deal with.

When I was done, the kids and teachers exited, and one teacher caught me and bent my ear with questions about hurricanes that she was curious about. As she was finally leaving, I noticed one other teacher sitting in the back.

"Mr. Sealls," he started, waving me toward him. "I have something personal I want to talk to you about." I was a little worried that he was going to chide me for saying something he perceived as anti-Christian or that he was going to query me on my religious views. "You don't know how much you've helped me today," he said, rising to extend his hand for a handshake. This man was White and in his late 30s. He seemed a little nervous and secretive. He looked around the room to make sure we were alone and then asked me to sit. I was relieved that he was complimenting me, and I figured that I had driven home a point to his students that he had often made.

Sitting fairly close to me on a pew, he clasped his hands and hung his head. "This is very hard for me. When I was ten years old, I was molested by two men, one Black and one White. I've only started to remember this in the last 5 years and my therapist says I should face it head on and talk about it."

I was more than surprised to hear this out of the blue.

"Until today, I've been afraid of you. I could never even watch you on TV. It took everything I had today to walk into this room."

I shook his hand and tried to tell him that I was happy to be able to help anybody, especially without even knowing it. I didn't ask any questions because I didn't want to know more. I did wonder though, when he said, "I've been afraid of you," whether he meant me specifically or all Black men. It's possible that I reminded him of one of his molesters. On the other hand, it's also possible that he harbored a fear of all Black men; and, unfortunately, that's understandable if by chance the only Black man he ever really knew as a child violated him.

Another teacher entered the room, but the man continued in a low voice to repeat how I made a difference in his life that I would never understand. I could only listen. After another half minute, I rose to leave and extended my hand again. He leaned toward me as though he wanted to embrace. In a split second I debated a hug, but I felt a firm handshake is always safer with strangers.

For the hundreds of presentations and events I've been invited to, many are initially awkward, like a blind date. Socially, I find myself in rooms filled with people who are of different educational, social, economic, religious, political, generational, ethnic, gender and philosophical backgrounds. People think they know me, because of my TV job, and often I know little about the organization or community where I'm speaking. Regardless of their expectation, just sharing my passion for weather, with corny jokes, has always worked out! Weather is one of the things most people agree on.

When I speak to groups, as long as it is a school, church, charitable organization, or an event that is open to the public, I've never asked for payment. I do presentations as a weather consultant or safety expert at businesses that are required to do employee safety training. For those, I charge. Otherwise, I'm quick to tell people that I cannot accept anything more than a token of appreciation. One church that I spoke to in Mobile gave me an unexpected cash token. At the end of my presentation, I was handed an envelope. I never open what people give me when I speak until I get home. Typically, the gift might be a gift card, but I was surprised at the large amount of the token in currency of multiple denominations. Unfortunately, the next day, an online news gossip site posted an insinuation that I requested payment. That made me look bad, and it made the event coordinator look bad. I learned that she did ask people who might attend the event for a donation, something that is standard practice at that church. Apparently, someone in the church misinterpreted those actions, and was either offended or unhappy with me and sent that to the gossip site.

Don't take my money

The 2009 economic downturn led to my corporate parent instituting a no-raise policy for employees and request for all contract employees to forego future raises. We were told how we all had to make difficult concessions in difficult times. One week later, the day before our responses to the pay freeze "request" were due, we were stunned again with another 10 layoffs of many veteran employees. I'm not sure if this was a coincidence or a well-timed ploy to create more fear in employees to make us more pliable. I was offended that after having negotiated a new personal services contract (PSC) the previous July, to which I gave my word and my company gave its word, now the company was "asking" me to redo the terms of the contract to benefit them. They offered a few things in return to all of us, but it was not worth the dollars I would lose.

A few days after this, I was talking to our human resources supervisor, next to the general manager's office, where a framed corporate "Core Values" statement hung. The frame was leaning to one side and one of the managers walked up to it, straightened it and said, "Our values are a little crooked." The general manager heard it and didn't smile. The human resources supervisor was surprised. The manager then realized what he really said, even though it wasn't how he meant it. They were the truest words he would end up speaking in a while!

I initially declined to "give" some of my pay back to the company, in a confidential decision. My managers pressed, coerced, and tried to embarrass me to be a "team player" and a "leader", when in reality they were really pleading for 100% compliance for their own job security. It got to the point that one manager approached me and, knowing there were other people within earshot, discussed my reluctance. That was a violation of my worker rights.

My agent heard through a corporate source that the company intended to release anyone who did not follow the request. Where I come from, that's called extortion. One of our young producers did not comply and she was released.

Upon advisement from my agent, and my wife, I acquiesced and signed the document. The same manager stopped by the weather office to express his satisfaction, with other people again in earshot. That was a calculated move on his part, to pressure others to follow. This, again, violated my confidentiality rights.

Working with snakes

At 5 minutes before news airtime, as I was sitting in the studio putting the last touches on my forecast, a reporter walked into the studio, froze, and yelled, "A SNAKE!" By his high-pitched tone I knew he was serious, so I cautiously got up and looked. Sure enough, right next to the anchor desk was a 12" (depending on who you ask) snake. Thanks to Hank from the local nature center having given me some of the basics on what to look for in venomous and non-venomous snakes, I boldly got a broom and started sweeping it out the door. It was non-venomous. I think the little thing even hissed at me, but I held my ground. My "courage" was further boosted by remembering what Hank said about the limited strike range of most snakes. My sports guy, Randy, the outdoorsman, said he thought it was a regular brown snake and helped to get it in a box. We released it outside.

Without Hank, there would have been no 10 pm news that night. I became the snake hero, at least until a 4-foot rattler shows up!

Just a pretty face

One of the other downsides of being on TV for me is having to wear makeup. Yes, I wear makeup. No, I don't like wearing makeup, and no, I don't wear it when I'm not on TV! Being in front of bright lights on TV that are aimed directly at your face requires, at a minimum, makeup to remove shine from oily skin. Translucent powder is all I wear. No lipstick, no mascara, no blush! A makeup consultant once gave me a full assessment. My foundation color is Egyptian Bronze, with an option of Golden Olive. My brows should be done with Black Coffee, and for touchup or bronzing, my "colour" is Big Bear. All of that came with an eleven-step instruction sheet. If anyone tried to follow it, it would have taken up half the time of a newscast! No thank you.

Makeup can change reality. Working one morning shift, arriving at work at 3 am, I saw a lady in the parking lot with glasses on and large rollers in her hair. I said hello. When she responded and I heard her voice, I realized it was a co-worker. Her makeup was always perfect, but it totally changed her natural appearance. Another woman I worked with, who was always made up for TV, I saw one day with no makeup. Her skin was beautiful, but I had never seen it before, beneath the veneer of cosmetics. She was so much more attractive. Yet another co-worker at a different station came to work with no makeup on, and one of the crew asked her if she was okay. Without her TV face, she looked like she was having an allergic reaction to something! Ouch!

When I worked at WGN and we had a makeup artist, I always avoided her. Like many makeup artists, she saw my face as a canvas, and she wanted to paint. Her intentions were good, to make me look natural on TV, but the outcome didn't work for me. Aside from using foundation and then a layer of makeup, she wanted to darken my eyebrows. If I feel any substance on my face, especially a veneer of makeup that can be scratched or rubbed off, I don't feel natural. If I look in the mirror, and don't recognize the guy, I definitely don't feel like me.

Men are held to a lower standard of cosmetic perfection than women are. That's not fair to women, but it has enabled me to get away with only wearing pressed powder, in minimal amounts. Pressed powder is a white matted powder that is colorless when applied to skin, and simply soaks up any excess oil to reduce shine. I've always worn so little that most people wouldn't even notice I'm wearing any in person. There was one time I bought the wrong powder. It had sparkles in it! I couldn't tell until I put it on. I threw that away quickly. It would not have worked very well on TV! I only want glitter in my personality!

My goal has always been to never look different or "better" on TV than in person. In other words, I've always wanted to look like me, an ordinary guy who has razor bumps, skin imperfections, and increasing wrinkles and graying hair. I don't ever want anyone who watches me to think that I'm superhuman, and different from any other professional who applies themself. There's already some of that, just based on the fact that I am trained as a scientist.

Unlike most scientists, I am also a performer and an artist, but not in the traditional definitions. Broadcast meteorology is a performing art in that we use spoken word, body language and graphics to tell a story. Effective speech alone is an art. Think of all the people you've seen deliver information, whether it was a teacher, preacher, politician, actor, singer, or even the flight attendant on an airline. Anybody can talk, but talking in a way that holds peoples' attention, and informs, is an art. It involves pacing, pausing, inflection, articulation, enunciation, and variation of delivery rate and volume. I've always tried to randomly include prose, alliteration, allusion, rhyme, rhythm, and humor, not just to entertain, but to grab the attention of viewers and make my delivery memorable and more effective.

I've developed a lot of "trademark" phrases which people seem to get a kick out of. Instead of saying we'll get rain, I'll say we'll hear the "pitter patter of raindrops on the rooftops." When lawns are drying up in a drought, the ground is "crunchy." In the still of summer, when humidity is high, I say, "step outside and the humidity will give you a hug." Weather that's comfortably warm is "roasty toasty." When dense fog creates a hazard, I remind people "when it's in your face, leave extra space." Yes, many of these are silly or corny but each has a purpose—to break the monotony of a weather presentation, get the listener to focus and remember something specific, at the same time hopefully giving them a smile or a chuckle.

Most of my unique phrases are spontaneous or sparked by hearing or reading something which I take to the next level. Inspiration comes often from music or literature. Other phrases come by listening to myself as I talk, through my ears. That's something I still do, to force me to articulate, soften a New York accent, and slow down!

Like many artists, whether they be visual artists, or musical artists, or even athletes, I am rarely happy with how I presented something. I always find something that I would have changed when I review past work. However, given that my work is ad lib, I know that no presentation will ever be perfect. My goal has always been to get close to that, though. I've had help, although not always in the way I like, from the various coaches and consultants that my stations have provided from time to time. I've had performance coaches who have pointed out mannerisms, posture, and delivery; wardrobe consultants who have come to my home and gone through my closet; and makeup consultants who see the world differently than I do. From each of them, I took a little advice but skipped a lot of it!

CHAPTER 9

My Late Career
Viral weather

Never in my life had I imagined I would go viral. It was never a goal or a plan or even a thought. Just like most viral things, it was more random luck and timing than anything unusual. In 2017, Hurricane Irma was one in a series of powerful and deadly hurricanes. There was high public interest in the tropics that hurricane season. While I didn't normally post my weather segments to my station's YouTube channel, because they were not often viewed until hours or days later, I did that summer for most of the significant hurricanes. I found that there was a large appetite for hurricane information from outside of my broadcast area.

On a typical YouTube weather forecast post, there might have been a few hundred views. On an active weather forecast, the views might have reached a few thousand. Over the course of a week, as I posted daily Hurricane Irma forecasts, the viewership went from around 5,000 initially to 25,000 within a couple of days. As Irma approached the United States, my daily views jumped to several hundred thousand, and then it happened… a man from the United Kingdom noticed one of the videos and made a post on Reddit about how thorough and understandable my forecast was, better than any he had ever seen before. The next day, I got an early morning call from my station's social media coordinator, J.B. "Hey Alan, you're trending on Reddit!" My response was, "What's Reddit?" At the time, I didn't know. Within hours, I was getting all sorts of messages and comments about my previous day's Hurricane Irma forecast. From family, friends, and colleagues, everyone was excited that I was going viral. That particular video went on to get 5 million views!

One of my colleagues, Marshall, later said very well what I was thinking about all that. He said that it was nothing unusual for me. The presentation was what I have always done throughout my career, just a longer version. In it, I tried to answer any question people might have about what Hurricane Irma was doing, where it was going, how we could determine that, what all the words and symbols meant, and what might change in the forecast. I would imagine that many people were disappointed in watching the video, that unlike most viral videos where something silly, dangerous, or embarrassing happens, mine was just solid, clear, science information.

Many articles and interviews followed. Most of all, I was pleased that people were happy that I represented my community, hometown, profession, and even ethnicity well. True to typical social media, there were some people who found fault or picked on trivial things about me, my delivery, and my appearance. Over that week, my videos became the majority of the all-time top-viewed videos on my station's YouTube channel, generating thousands of dollars for the station. No, I did not get a raise or a bonus. I did get a trophy!

The week afterward, I did a Reddit AMA (Ask Me Anything). That is a live online question and answer session Reddit coordinates with celebrities, professionals and high-visibility people in entertainment, politics, science, business, news, sports, or some other arena. From around the world, I was peppered with questions about going viral, meteorology, TV, racism, and life in general, along with a bunch of silly but fun topics. My AMA ranked among the top ten of Reddit AMAs for many years!

This was gratifying. A new generation was exposed to my work. It was sort of like when I was a kid, discovering an old vinyl record album in my parents' closet with classic music that was awesome. It was there all along, but I had never noticed!

Legal weather

Trying to maintain high standards of award-worthy work also led to me being pulled into the field of forensic meteorology. That's the use of weather in legal matters, typically something as simple as answering the question, "What was the weather?" on a particular day and time at a specific location. For most of my career, I avoided that sort of work as it can end up in a courtroom, and I did not want to be perceived by the public as taking sides in a legal case.

After multiple calls from attorneys, I dipped my toes into the field. I found that most lawsuits involving weather do not go to trial. They settle. I also found that my credentials and accomplishments made me ideal for attorneys. Not only was I perceived to be an expert meteorologist and weather communicator, I actually was! That grew from the combination of holding a higher degree, multiple certifications, dozens of awards and recognitions, becoming president of two different national organization, being an adjunct professor for decades, regularly presenting at conferences to my peers, producing over one hundred independent educational weather videos, writing for a newspaper, going viral on YouTube for an intelligent, comprehendible hurricane forecast viewed by millions, and most importantly, being able to take complex data and make it simple for the average person to understand. All of that makes me a credible weather expert in any courtroom. These are all things that came together organically, just from my love of meteorology.

It was a huge adjustment to learn the protocols and lingo of the legal profession. Given the high dollar amounts of claims, and the finality of court rulings, this was a bit intimidating, until I put in perspective that nobody can say exactly what happened in the past if they were not there. We can only do our best, and that's what I did. In most of the cases, my report or testimony was not the sole deciding factor.

Another big adjustment for me was going from the rapid pace of TV news to the slow pace of the legal system, where things can drag on. There was one hurricane-related case which I thought I was done with. Months later I found out that the case wasn't resolved, and I ended up in court as an expert witness. I had not set foot in a courtroom in 35 years. The last time that I had been in a courtroom was in Albany, Georgia, where I was working a shift as a photographer during a murder trial. I made the mistake of walking into the courtroom during testimony, to talk to a reporter, upsetting the room, for which I was later chided by the judge. The judge followed that with a smile, saying that he watched me on TV. Since then, as a member of the media, I've only been called once for jury duty, and I was excused.

A week before a case in which I provided weather data and interpretation to the defendant, where he was accused of negligence in allowing his property to be blown by wind to impact and damage someone else's home in a hurricane, I was subpoenaed to testify as an expert witness. My report was similar to that of the plaintiff's meteorologist, so neither of us had done a deposition. There was no real dispute about the weather events. I certainly wasn't expecting to be called in to testify. Two other co-defendants had settled just days earlier.

The defendant's attorney (my side) was fairly new to me. Initially I had worked with a group of other attorneys for the consulting and writing of a report. They knew more about me from being local. This new attorney was from a different city. We spent days going over the basics of what I should expect and be prepared for. I needed to know the content of the report that I had written, and then be able to reference content from a large NOAA report. I knew that the plaintiff's attorney would be asking me questions about both, but I didn't know what the questions would be! That's like studying for a final exam. You can't just memorize the key facts; you have to actually know them.

I was subpoenaed to appear at 9 am, but not told what time I would likely be called to testify. That set me up for a potential conflict with working my evening shift as a TV chief meteorologist. Fortunately, my boss was understanding, and we put someone on standby to work for me, in case the trial held me late. One of the rules of being in court is that I could not have my cell phone with me so that presented a possible communications issue.

After working my TV job on the day prior to court, I managed to get a reasonable night's sleep, which is hard enough because I had to go to bed and wake up two hours earlier than my normal sleep schedule. Since the trial was on a regular workday, I wore my uniform of a suit and tie. I purposely chose a combination of a dark suit, and a solid tie to be conservative, but professional. I avoided my regular ties which are a little more attention-getting. I got to the Federal Courthouse and got through security. Upon taking the elevator to the third floor, I followed the instructions to make a left, go down the hall, and then enter the small room to the left of the courtroom. Those instructions failed to tell me that I had to first enter the outer chamber doors of the courtroom to find the small room! Fortunately, as I wandered around, I finally saw my attorney and she escorted me in. She was focused but not worried. I reminded myself that this was as routine to her as covering a tornado warning was to me, where most people would be overwhelmed by the number of things that must happen, in a precise order.

She briefed me again, and before leaving the room, said someone would come out and get me when it was my turn. Luckily for me, I had brought a few magazines to read. They were unrelated to the case or to weather, so that I could let my mind relax. I got up, walked around a few times, went to the restroom, and then later stood to stay awake and alert. After two hours, I was called.

One of the plaintiff's attorneys summoned me, which seemed a little odd because he was the opposition. Walking me toward the courtroom, he introduced himself and reminded me with a smile that I had met him at a Rotary Club meeting where I was the speaker. I entered the courtroom. A modern, narrow room with a high ceiling. The bailiff swung open the small half-height door from the gallery to where the attorneys and court staff and bench were located. I didn't know where to go, so I made eye contact with the court clerk, who was standing. She motioned for me to go to the witness stand. I didn't know if I had to put my hand on a Bible or not. I didn't! She had me raise my right hand and agree to tell the truth. I did. Then I sat, trying to reorient myself. This was a bench trial, meaning there was no jury. The plaintiff's attorneys were in the middle of the room, closer to the gallery than to the stand. They were pretty far away. My attorneys were to my right, halfway between the plaintiff and the judge. Immediately in front of the judge were the court reporter, deputy, and judge's clerk. I had a Plexiglass barrier in front of me, maybe leftover from Covid precautions. Immediately in front of me was a microphone, and a large computer monitor on which I would see the exhibits the attorneys referenced.

Just as the opposing attorney was about to start his examination. I realized that I had not acknowledged the judge. I wasn't sure whether I should greet him or just stare straight ahead. I turned and looked at him, nodded, and softly said hello. He responded.

The attorney started by asking me to state my name, occupation, and verify that the report displayed as exhibit was mine. I affirmed. In an attempt to soften me up, he congratulated me on my announced retirement from TV. For a few minutes he asked me simple questions in which I verified that I either wrote parts of the report, or I clarified what certain exhibits represented. No question was hard. There were some weather questions that did not have yes/no answers and those were tricky because I had to explain why that was the case, without opening myself up to other lines of questioning.

As expected, the plaintiff's attorney asked me questions about my opinion, beyond what was in the report I prepared, and my attorney immediately objected. The judge overruled, stating that they were commonsense questions. My attorney cross-examined me, and then the opposing attorney had a few more questions before I was done. He asked me a question that was not in my report but related to storm preparation advice I always give people on social media. I didn't see that coming. It was a score for the plaintiff. I half-smiled at his cleverness. Just as I thought I was done, the judge asked me a weather question. I didn't know that was going to happen either! It wasn't a hard question, but it was one that did not have a solid, single answer. I took a long pause before answering to make sure my phrasing was correct and direct.

That was it. Through the entire proceedings, I tried to not make myself the center of attention, although I could see some of the court staff smiling and trying to make eye contact with me, as a local "celebrity." I left the courtroom, returned to my prep room, and waited for my attorney to release me. That's when I finally and first met the defendant who hired the attorney who hired me. He said he was a regular viewer of mine. The defendant was unsuccessful, but that had no bearing on my consulting fee. Facts are facts.

Changing stations

After being in Mobile for nearly 20 years, with multiple contracts at the station that originally hired me, that ended. It was not my plan, and it was not about money. I was looking for a better work schedule for me, and a better work environment for me and my co-workers. Management wanted me to do things that I didn't want to do, and I wanted them to do things that they were unwilling to do. I didn't quit. I wasn't fired. We separated. I walked away, knowing that I could easily get another job, but also knowing that I had enough savings and professional projects that I would not hurt. It was a big deal for the community. People had gotten so used to seeing me at that station, and people don't like change.

It came as a shock to the public and my co-workers because no one saw it coming. My contract expired while I was at a weather conference in San Diego. I had hoped to have things wrapped up before I left but my previous company was moving slowly. I was prepared for either outcome, so before I got on the plane to leave for California, I recorded a farewell message for my YouTube channel, but I didn't post it. After some more back and forth negotiating between my agent and my former station, ending in an impasse, I reiterated that I would not sign the new contract as they had offered. The station put out a press release saying that I was leaving, "to spend more time with family." That wasn't true. I knew when they posted it because in a conference session, people started looking at me, and then asking what was going on! I stepped out of the session, and posted my video, thanking the viewers for their support. I explained that I wasn't sick, and I wasn't leaving Mobile, or retiring, and that I would probably be back on TV at some point.

Within several days, I had half a dozen job offers from within Mobile and from elsewhere. The week after I got back, my agent had set up informal talks with a couple of stations. I had no intention of moving for a job, at this late stage of my career, so I never considered jobs elsewhere. Colleagues and friends reached out to me with suggestions and even offers. One of the best and funniest comments I got was from Rob, a veteran chief meteorologist in another city: "Any market would be lucky to get you but stay the f#@k out of my market!" I ended up choosing the NBC affiliate in Mobile for the same position of chief meteorologist.

By my recently ended job contract, I had a 6-month non-compete. That's a period where I could not work at another TV station in Mobile that was competition to my old station. That was no problem. It was a plus to have time off to focus on me and family. I continued my social media projects and interaction, as well as community appearances. The transition to the new station was not too hard. I had a lot of friends who worked there or had worked there. My biggest adjustment was to the weather graphics system. It was a different brand and design from what I had just worked with. Starting in January of 2020, I picked up where I left off, as a chief meteorologist in Mobile, and then came Covid.

Covid storm

The week of the Covid lockdown, I had what would be my last airplane flight for a long time. It was Super Tuesday primary election day in March of 2020. I got a call around 8 am from my boss. I normally don't wake up until 10 am. "Corporate wants to know if you can go to Nashville today. They had tornadoes last night, and their chief meteorologist is out of town." It was a day when the Mobile area had a slight threat of severe weather. Given that and given that I just did not want to go, I responded, "Not really. Can they find someone else?" My boss said he would check back. I laid back down to try to sleep. Minutes later the phone rings. "We've got you a ticket to Nashville for a noon flight. You'll probably be there a couple of days." So much for having a choice! The decision was made for me. I got up. Went to my station to get my makeup and earpiece, rushed to go vote, and then grabbed a couple of suits, before heading to the airport.

By 6 pm that day, I was on the air at our sister station in Nashville, covering the aftermath of devastating tornadoes. Fortunately, the station had the same equipment as mine, and I had access to my corporate email and other accounts. Also fortunate is that, with family in Nashville, I had a reasonable understanding of the geography. Given all the hurdles, I was satisfied in that I did a good job, giving the viewers perspective on what happened, and correctly identifying and pronouncing communities. I got a lot of positive comments, but also comments of confusion by people in Nashville and people in Mobile, who couldn't figure out why I was there!

The day after I returned to Mobile, the Covid lockdown was put in place. The world turned upside down. We were in the routine of wearing face masks, social distancing, and wiping down our work areas with cleaning wipes. Early on, I noticed a couple of evenings in a row that when I got home, my throat was sore. I didn't otherwise feel bad, but I did not want to potentially pass on an illness to my co-workers. I decided to work from home. Given remote computer access and broadcast apps, the workflow was not too hard. After two days of not having a sore throat, I realized why my throat was getting sore. The wipes we used at work had a high bleach content and odor. In the process of wiping wide counter spaces, those vapors got to me! I had my station switch to a different brand of wipes and then went back to work, to a very empty building.

Once the Covid vaccines became available, I made a decision to post a picture of me getting mine. I never want to make myself the center of attention, and I definitely never share personal medical information, but I felt this was important—life-or-death important. I used my power as a trusted scientist and community member to make the statement that the vaccine was common-sense safety. I got a few negative comments but 99% of the comments were highly supportive of me and the vaccine. As Covid lingered, I authored this article as one of my newspaper weather columns:

Hurricane Corona: That's a bad thought, that there's a hurricane named Corona. In a sense, there was. COVID-19, aka coronavirus, was historic, in a bad way. In the spring of 2020, the looming pandemic was a lot like hearing that a category 5 hurricane was in the Caribbean, devastating countries and seemingly on a track to us. Days later, you heard that the arrival was certain, and you were advised to prepare. When it arrived, you were told to hunker down. The coronavirus impact had a lot in common with the impact of a hurricane.

In 2020, in the United States, around 500 people were killed by hurricanes and extreme weather, according to NOAA. Around 350,000 were killed by COVID-19, according to CDC.

By the way, corona is defined as something with a crown-like structure, or as the glow around bright objects. Corona describes the glow of fuzzy color around a bright moon when we have middle-level clouds called altocumulus clouds. The CDC says the corona virus was so-named because under a microscope, a single virion has a corona.

Like a hurricane, there was coronavirus misinformation, speculation, and pontification on social media and from the loud-talking non-experts, six feet in front of you at the store. Just like with a hurricane threat, we saw government leaders in daily press conferences with their support agencies behind them. The message was the same. Prepare. Don't panic. Use common sense.

In a hurricane, we hear criteria like a hurricane warning stopping at the state line. Does that mean that the impact of the storm will be total on one side of the line and zero on the other? No. Those lines are general boundaries based on geographical markers that people understand. If you are told to stay 6 feet away from someone to limit the spread of a virus, does that mean that if you are 6 feet, 1 inch away that you are safe but at 5 feet,

11 inches away you are certain to contract a virus? No, 6 feet is a rough number. Follow the advice of the 80s hit from the Police, 'Don't stand so close to me'.

As during a hurricane, trust the experts, starting with your physician. Respect the doctors and medical officials who have dedicated their lives and professions to health and safety. Just as in a hurricane, where meteorologists cannot tell you exactly how long a storm will sit in one spot, or what it will do to your house, medical professionals cannot do that for the coronavirus because this particular one has never happened before, and none has spread as fast as far in modern history. This virus started off moving at spurts of 500 mph via air travel.

Like a major hurricane can spawn a new generation of meteorologists, my hope is that this pandemic will inspire young people to pursue science, biology, epidemiology, and find vaccines and cures. We hope to never deal with more pandemics, but history and the present have shown that they do happen.

This unprecedented coronavirus pandemic is like a hurricane in that it shut down society for an unforeseeable length of time. It still requires caution, patience, a positive attitude, and community togetherness. Like the bands of a hurricane can be devastating to select areas, while others escape the worst, most of us will get through this without major issues. That doesn't mean you should have a hurricane party, where you disregard threats, and put first responders at risk. Most of us have friends and family who are impacted and maybe devastated, *if not deceased, by COVID-19. Families, businesses, and countries have taken huge financial blows.*

Just as Hurricane Sally was an excruciatingly slow-moving storm, we are now in the eye of the slow-moving Hurricane Corona storm. Looking at how doctors and researchers have handled data collection from multiple sources, computer model and model ensemble projections, communicating with the public and being second-guessed by non-professionals, I see exactly what we meteorologists go through when a storm, with extreme metrics that we've only theorized in the past, arrives. Don't blame the messenger.

In the eye of the storm, the winds are calm, the sun beams and neighbors emerge from shelter. If you've been in the eye of a hurricane, then you know the calm is misleading. It is only the halfway point. The worst is not necessarily over. Winds will shift as the second half of the storm takes hold, with possibly greater force and threat to recently weakened infrastructure.

Take the hurricane analogy a step further. Think back to Hurricane Ivan, in 2004. After the eye traveled through Baldwin County, and later exited Alabama, Ivan took a northward path along the Appalachians. The remnants moved out to the Atlantic. A portion of them got caught up in a different steering wind, pushing them southward, then westward, for a return to the Gulf of Mexico, to make another landfall in Louisiana. That scared and confused many of us, but it relates to the reality of the Coronavirus Delta variant.

Projections of the pandemic are sure to change, as do projections of a hurricane. However, in a hurricane, we have no control over the magnitude and duration of the storm. In a pandemic, human actions do play into the extent and duration of the impact. Be wise. Be safe.

That article space in *Lagniappe Newspaper* is called Weather Things. Meteorology is the focus. One more time I deviated from that.

The sky is blue, my skin is brown

After the killing of George Floyd in 2020 by police officers, I used my platform to educate, but not about weather. I wrote this article in my newspaper column and shared it on social media:

Each day, before I become a meteorologist, I wake up a human being. On some days, at some point, something reminds me that I'm an African American man. My parents raised me with that awareness and a solid understanding of American history, so I've been fortunate to not have had my life directly threatened by someone who fears or disregards my skin color. I'm acutely aware that in an instant that could change. I've experienced multiple situations that tell me how I am often perceived. Here are just a few:

As a teen, I walked into a sewing store to purchase fabric. Everyone froze and looked at me. The owner stopped what he was doing and hurriedly served me so that I could quickly be out of the store.

On winter break from college, in a brief conversation with a White woman on the streets of New York City, she asked, "What college do you go to?" "Cornell," I replied, proudly. Her response: "No you don't," and she turned and walked away.

In Chicago, after leaving the meteorology course I taught at Columbia College, I walked to a hotel cab stand to hail a cab. The cab driver looked at me and then pulled off.

In West Mobile, while cutting the grass at my home, I was mistaken by an elderly White man to be 'the yardman,' not the homeowner.

In Boston, visiting my brother, we were standing outside his home. A young Black man sped by. A few moments later, a White police officer raced to the area. My brother and I pointed in the direction that the young man went. The officer rolled his eyes and turned to go in the other direction.

In St. Louis in 2019, for the annual meeting of the National Weather Association, I was serving as the first Black president in the organization's 43-year history. I went to dinner with a friend, a White woman. In the restaurant was a bicycle police officer. He glanced at my friend, then looked at me, sizing me up. I made eye contact, smiled, nodded my head, and said, 'Hello.' He turned away without response, denying my existence, denying my humanity.

Those are the days I do not like. They are annoying and frustrating, but routine for so many brown-skinned people in the United States. I could recount worse incidents that my family and Black friends faced where their welfare was put at risk by someone charged with enforcing the law.

I share these to provide perspective of why our country is in turbulence, following the death of George Floyd during a police encounter. As an educator and broadcast meteorologist, I want everyone to be more aware and educated to contribute to a more equitable, healthy, and safe society, in all regards.

The sky is blue, my skin is brown, but I am optimistic. After the turbulence, inconvenience, and destruction of a storm, comes renewal and balance. With a shift in the wind, fresh air will allow all of us to breathe.

The article was widely shared and supported on my social media, where the majority of my followers appear to be White, and most of those are women. I often think that many of us live in bubbles of people who are like ourselves, and have little first-hand knowledge of how others live their lives. I've been asked if my ethnicity has played a role in my career advancement or lack of advancement. My answer is, "Yes and no," but I don't know when it did either. I know that in my academic endeavors and within my professional life, I've been the first Black man in many areas. I've also been the only Black man in many situations. "Only" rhymes with "lonely" and sometimes the two can be interchanged. Being the first Black man was never a thought or a goal for me. My intention has been and remains to be the best meteorologist, period, not just the first or best Black one. I also don't want to be the last Black one.

In that George Floyd article, I left out many of the microaggressions that I've dealt with, like when I was an AMS Councilor, recently selected as a Fellow. Being named a Fellow is a high honor for substantial and impactful contribution to the profession, those of us in it, and those served by it. I've always donated to the AMS, and therefore receive an invitation to a donor's reception at the annual conference. Traditionally, the donors are older, White members with disposable income. That never bothered me, but it was important for me to be there and show that all members make financial contributions. As is normal for me, I walked briskly and confidently into the reception room and recognized some colleagues. Before I could reach any of them, a conference staff person behind me says, "Excuse me?" It was not the friendly tone of, "Do we know each other?" It was a sharp tone of, "You must be lost, you don't seem to belong here." I greeted her with a handshake, wearing my badge with Councilor and Fellow ribbons and introduced myself. She prejudged me. She was caught off-guard and couldn't say much.

The toughest days of my career

You might think the hardest days of my broadcast career were weather incidents where there was tremendous destruction, injury, and death. The toughest day was something like that, but it was not weather-related. It was 9/11 in 2001, when terrorists hijacked airplanes, destroyed the World Trade Center towers and killed several thousand innocent people.

I remember being awakened mid-morning by my wife who had just answered a phone call from my oldest brother, Eric. Eric was working in Manhattan a few miles north of the twin towers. He told her to turn on the TV. She asked, "Which channel?" He said, "Any channel." I got out of bed and watched in disbelief and confusion like everyone else. I saw the second plane hit the towers but none of it made any sense. It was surreal, but at least my brother was okay.

By evening, the loss of life and terrorist connection were being put together. I wanted to cry and scream. I had nothing to smile about, but I had to do my job, delivering weather on TV … and I did, but I don't remember it, probably on purpose.

November 4, 2008. Election Day. John McCain vs. Barak Obama. This was my second hardest day, working in TV. Through the entire campaigning period, I knew that there were never before the right ingredients to allow a Black man to become president of the United States of America. Obama was my choice, not just because he was Black. At work, preparing for the 10 pm news, exit poll data arrived showing Obama ahead. I froze and made sure that I wasn't misreading the data. A few minutes later, CBS news goes to scenes of celebrations on Black college campuses and then to their broadcast studios with reporter Byron Pitts. Byron showed what I was feeling ... overcome by emotion he held up a picture of his grandmother (I believe) and talked about what the likely win by Obama meant to her and other Black folks who had struggled in life-long fights for equality. I wanted to cry and scream but unlike 9/11 this would have been for joy, not just for me and my ancestors and family, but for the United States finally putting our constitution into action and showing the world that even the underclass or perceived underclass has the opportunity to overcome.

I was inspired and overjoyed, but in my Republican State of Alabama, and in my place of employment where many of my co-workers had never finished college, and in my profession of journalism where we are supposed to project an image of neutrality and non-bias, I had to hold it all in. That was tough. In my weather segment I wanted to say something, anything, to let the viewers know how happy I was that Obama would become the 44th President, but I couldn't.

Surprise layoffs

My phone showed a missed morning phone call from Bob, my news director. I was asleep and he didn't leave a voice message, but he did leave a text asking me to call him back. I don't get many calls like that, so I knew it was important, and surmised something negative was going on. I was too groggy to connect a clue that was presented three weeks earlier. Our corporate heads held an annual state-of-the-company video meeting. They talked about all initiatives and projects but didn't mention local TV news. That was a sign, but not one that was unexpected. Local TV news had been on the decline for years. We were told at the end of the previous year that the company was preparing for a recession. Two weeks prior to the call, there was news of some of our sister stations having layoffs. That was clue number two. Some of the staff were concerned, as they should have been, but local management didn't expect anything to impact us. The morning phone call proved that wrong.

When I called back, our conversation started with, "Alan, you're okay, but we've had layoffs." The newsroom had already met and gotten the news that people would be cut. It turned out that the majority of our news department was cut, by corporate decree. We were dropping newscasts and scaling down to work with the absolute minimum. Many of my co-workers, in their 20s, for whom this was their first job in broadcasting, were devastated. They had never gone through a layoff before, and it was a shock. A few had already been planning to move on to other or bigger things, but the majority were blindsided. Even for those remaining, it was not a good feeling to see all of your friends disappear. It was like being the last house standing in a community after a hurricane wipes out the neighbors. At the same time, many of us knew that with a skeleton staff, we survivors would be working harder than ever.

Layoffs are not unique to TV news—they are always a possibility in any corporate-owned or independent company. That, along with changes in technology, and consumer demand, is the reason why nobody can assume their job will always exist. Have a plan B. My weather team was cut from 3 to 2, and my cut colleague reminded me that I had told him when he was a student that getting let go in a layoff is a badge of honor, rather than something shameful due to poor job performance. That's a positive way to look at it, if you have savings and options, as he did. He ended up being hired shortly after that as a chief meteorologist. Nearly everyone else who had been laid off also found equal or better jobs, although some had to move. That is part of any career. A layoff can be the kick that forces you to jump, move, and grow, but you must be skilled and marketable.

That same month was also my first photo exhibit. I had never considered a public display of my weather photos, simply because it just never crossed my mind. I had always taken pictures for enjoyment, for education, to use in my video productions, and to license to others who wanted to use them. A colleague at the university library where I teach had seen some of my photos, after I contacted her for guidance on publishing a weather photo book. She immediately asked me to do an exhibit in the library art gallery. After Covid pandemic delays, it happened and I was pleased. My exhibit, *Weather Things in Photos: The Art and Science of the Atmosphere*, gave me the opportunity to share things that were important to me with others. It made a big difference to me to take photos that only existed as digital files on my computer and have them framed and hung on a wall, where I could look at them from a distance. The lesson I learned applies to all artists—let others see or hear your work, so that you can learn how valuable or significant it is or isn't! More importantly, art can inspire and educate. By the way, art can generate revenue.

I don't post many of my photos online, for fear that people will take them and use them without compensation to me. If I do post one of mine, I put my name on it. Once a photo goes on social media, you lose control, even though you have copyright protection. Enforcing copyright can be costly, requiring the work of attorneys. I'm more than happy to share a good weather photo that someone else captured, especially when it shows something unique or just really pretty. It's then not unusual for someone else to reply with or send me a photo without any comment. What I don't like is when I later find that it is an old picture, or a picture taken somewhere else in the world by someone else. This causes confusion for me, and for anyone else looking at the photo. In the haste of completing daily job tasks, it's critical to verify that any image you show or share is what it claims or suggests to be. Sometimes, people create an artistic or fantasy image of weather that is taken and then circulated online as though it is real.

Sonic booming questions

Every once in a while, my Facebook page lights up with, "What was that boom?" On the central Gulf Coast, periodically people may hear a series of extremely loud explosions, followed by rattles and shakes that would lead them to believe they are experiencing an earthquake. Some people run outside looking for signs of an airplane crash, thinking something may have landed on their roof. Dogs and other animals may react dramatically. Without fail, on social media, dozens of people will proclaim it was an earthquake, while dozens more argue it was not. A handful of people propose conspiracy theories. The majority of people accept it is a likely sonic boom. That's what I do if the United States Geological Survey does not detect an earthquake, after a loud boom and shake across a county or two, on a sunny day, when no business or facility reports an explosion.

Consider the substantial number of military aircraft that traverse airspace, in and out of the multiple central Gulf Coast air bases. They are not supposed to break the sound barrier near land, but just like you find yourself "accidentally" speeding, it shouldn't surprise anyone that a pilot might do the same. I would guess a pilot might hope that no one noticed either! Our military rarely confirms when this happens, in part because it might also be secret testing to strengthen our defenses or capabilities. There are also times when a pilot creates a brief sonic boom but may be unaware.

After any boom, I double-check satellite to make sure there were no thunderstorms. I also check weather radar for a signature of "chaff," tiny metallic particles released from airplanes to cloak aircraft from radar detection, suggesting that some type of exercise is ongoing. That's not unusual on the Gulf Coast.

A sonic boom is generated and distributed according to flight speed, altitude, angle, direction, descent or ascent, and what type of aircraft it is. A sonic boom will be modified if there are multiple planes breaking the sound barrier at the same time. What you hear or feel in a sonic boom will depend upon the type of building you are in (brick, wood, steel); whether it is elevated on pilings; how tall it is (ranch, multi-story, high-rise); what floor you are on; and from which way the sonic boom approaches. Sound travels farther on cold, calm mornings when dense air sinks to the ground. The atmosphere can channel and focus sound. Sonic booms are pressure waves or shock waves, just like those from lightning or explosions. If you feel something in your ears, it is from rapid pressure change. That's similar to when you have two windows open in your vehicle at highway speed, and you get pulsating air pressure that hurts your ears.

Please help me

Seemingly every day, someone contacts me with a task. They either want me to research something for them, or they want me to appear at an event, or speak to a group. A lady called me while helping her child do her homework, asking me, "What is a barometer?" My thought was, "What is a dictionary?" I didn't say that aloud! I was dismayed that a parent would show their child that the quick way to getting an answer to a question is calling someone who works on TV. The lesson for the child should have been to look it up in a dictionary, or online.

My job has never been to do other people's homework. I had another lady call me and ask, since I had worked in Chicago, if I could help her find her long-lost sister from there. No. It's flattering that people have that much trust and respect for me, but you have to learn to say no and set boundaries. One of my boundaries is that I don't return a call to someone who leaves a message but doesn't identify themself or give a clear reason for why they called, yet they want me to call them back. That's clearly someone who wants something from me. If you want or need something from someone, when you leave a message, tell them what it is.

Teachers and parents always want you to speak to their kids, and they sometimes get indignant if they see that you spoke at one school, but not theirs. Given my shrinking time and energy in my late-career stage, the boundaries are more defined. I don't speak to kindergarten or first graders, because they don't really know who I am, and any guest speaker with visuals would be just as effective. I generally speak to third grade and up because the kids are a bit more mature and attentive; and because third grade is typically the grade where they undertake a formal weather unit, so they get much more out of my presentation than the little kids would.

I had to stop doing single-class presentations in person because it takes a lot of time and energy to speak to a small group of kids, when you could reach more by talking to an entire grade, or multiple grades. This is especially true when the same teachers invite you back each year. It sometimes takes effort to keep order with larger groups but one of my tricks has always been to take the most disruptive kids and have them help me do experiments, to remove them from being a distraction, but also to show them that they can get attention by doing positive things. I also choose a shy or an attentive kid to help me, in order to give them a spotlight and boost their self-esteem.

I'm invited to be master of ceremony to events because organizations think that my name will attract an audience, or they've heard that I tend to be an engaging and humorous presenter. That's wonderful except that some events last several hours and are just boring. Other events have a long script for me to read, often with names of people that I can't pronounce. That's challenging and awkward. What's even worse is when I'm invited to an event to perform a task and the organizers are unorganized and fail to get the written material to me until the last minute, and then give no direction. It's never a good sign when they spell my name wrong on the program! For those reasons, I avoid being master of ceremony, unless I know it's a well-oiled operation, for an event that is fun, and short!

I've received the honor of being an invited speaker at universities and conferences. Those are almost always well-coordinated. Educators and professionals think I have something important to share, I'd like to think, in a way that is informative, educational, and entertaining.

That's similar to the interviews I've contributed to or been the subject of. Some high school kids even wrote a book about me and my career, called *Capturing the Sky: The True Story of How Alan Sealls Became the Best Weatherman Ever*. That's a compliment.

CHAPTER 10

The Viewers Speak
The good, the bad, the ugly, and the weird.

When I was hired at WKRG-TV in 1999, the station was in the beginning of a long push to make weather their brand. It was successful. Part of that effort meant aggressive severe weather coverage. At the time, this was new to the Mobile area, and people were very upset when programs were interrupted. They often called to complain. Being the new kid on the block, I got a large share of complaints, some of which directly or indirectly referenced my ethnicity. I've found that when people are upset, they lash out and release their life's frustrations, to childishly pick on people in any way that that person is different from them. Throughout my career, this has been consistent. The majority of offenders are men. From the anonymity of a phone call, email or social media post, many men bully and intimidate, in a way that they would not do to a stranger, face to face. It's like road rage for TV, so I call it "remote rage."

In covering severe weather, on a December afternoon in 2009, a squall line came through in the late afternoon with isolated tornado warnings. I do a program cut-in at 3:45 pm near the end of "Reba". The phone rings as soon as I get off the air. I don't answer it since I know it's usually an upset viewer. A few minutes later, I check the message and from the first sentence I confirm my suspicions. I've also learned to not listen to the full message until after the bad weather is past, otherwise my mood is dragged downward by negativity. Later, I listen to a man named Sam who works at a trucking company complain that I "showed my ass," while interrupting the end of his show to announce a tornado *watch*. He left his number. Sam was wrong in that it was a tornado *warning*, and for that my station policy was to cut in and announce so that viewers who may be vision-impaired will get information.

Three days later, I called "Sam". The phone rang. A lady answered. I identified myself, "Hi, this is Alan Sealls from channel 5 returning a call to Sam." She hesitated, "Uh, wait a minute." I hear her talking to someone in the background. A man gets on the phone, with the same distinct voice that I recalled from the voicemail. Again, I identify myself and ask, "Is this Sam?" Abruptly he says, "No, there's no Sam here," and hangs up. I laughed. He was so embarrassed that I called him back he couldn't say anything. I would never hear from him again, and that was part of my goal.

When the weather has been quiet for long periods and I've had to interrupt the program for a tornado warning, people become more upset than if we had just had destructive or deadly weather recently. By the comments on social media and email, many of which are anonymous, it's clear to me that people make me, the messenger, their target to pick on or pick apart, in my attempts to fulfil my job. Imagine a job where strangers critique, criticize, berate, and belittle you for doing what your company pays you to do. That's what many weather broadcasters go through, and it is far worse for women broadcasters.

These are just some of the comments we get during severe weather on TV. Why are you breaking into my program? I don't care about bad weather somewhere else. You always do this when my favorite show is on. Why don't you just wait until a commercial or put the words on the bottom of the screen? Can't you just say it in 30 seconds and get back to the program? Just put it on your other channel. The other stations are not on with the weather, why are you? You keep repeating the same thing over and over. My county never gets mentioned when there is bad weather. You said it was going to be bad, but nothing happened.

When people contact me with complaints, and any sort of question, even if it was rhetorical, I've always responded. Even when they attack me, I respond, except I wait a few days until they calm down and I'm in a better mood. Typically, when I point out or repeat what they said to me, they apologize for being rude or using a poor choice of words. I respond to educate them, but I also respond so they know they cannot bully or harass and expect to get away with it. It works! If they email me, I've often responded with a long description, like this one.

Every TV station has a policy for covering tornado threats. It's not a decision made only by a meteorologist. The FCC (Federal Communications Commission) requires local commercial TV broadcasters to put emergency information on TV both audibly and visibly with an alert tone to get your attention. In order for a TV station to maintain an FCC broadcast license, this must be a consistent practice on the broadcaster's main channel since not all cable or satellite providers carry sub-channels. We must deliver details about what and where the threat is within our coverage area, and what individuals need to do to be safe. This information must be available to hearing-impaired or vision-impaired people. There is no technology right now that allows us to only inform people in affected areas of a weather hazard. There are projects underway that will hopefully soon make this possible.

When a twister will drop from the sky is not as easy to predict as you might think. A broadcaster who waits to make an announcement of a tornado only after it is confirmed or a broadcaster who goes off the air too quickly risks missing that tornado and puts lives in jeopardy. During a program interruption, the meteorologist is not just announcing what is happening, he or she is looking at the radar trend and other incoming data to make sure that they don't prematurely end that announcement and have to interrupt the program again for the same storm or a new storm. It takes several minutes to receive a complete radar update. We continually repeat and update information for viewers who may just be tuning in, and for the visitors to our region who are not as familiar as local residents with locations or safety procedures. As people channel surf, it's important for them to get the full story at whatever point they may join in.

Since tornado warnings fall into the category of emergency, it would make no sense to hold the information until a commercial or for any length of time. Forecasters watch the radar, so trying to figure out where a program is in the storyline is not practical. Many programs air again on satellite or cable providers' on-demand section. For tornado warnings, every TV station I know of does interrupt commercials and lose revenue in the process, as part of the commitment to serving the public. Since commercials are shorter than the programs, most people only notice when the program is interrupted.

After the fact, anybody can say nothing happened, but during the moment, no one can say there is no tornado. Broadcasters weigh the threat of danger with the entertainment value of a television program and with FCC requirements and advertiser commitments. It may be sunny and calm where you are, while a family in another county may be huddling in fear for their safety. If a potential tornado were approaching your mother's house in a different county and you wanted to watch your favorite show, what would you want the TV station to do?

Why other stations do or don't cut in and announce a particular tornado is a decision that is up to their management. It would be a bad thing if no TV station in a city delivers emergency information just because the others are not doing so. No human can control when weather emergencies occur but, when there's a potential tornado threat in your community, meteorologists strive to ensure that you, your family, and your neighbors know about it without hype. Severe weather is never convenient, not for you and not for us.

If you want to talk with me regarding how I can cover your weather better, call me on a sunny day, not when a storm is moving through the area. Please do not yell, cuss, call me names or talk to me like I'm a child, and I'll never do the same to you. Give me the respect and opportunity to respond instead of just saying what you want and hanging up. If you leave a voice message, give your name and phone number.

True complaints, with spelling, grammar, and punctuation exactly as they were sent.

+++

Tornado warning interruption, complaint: What is not necessary and is certainly outdated in our current digital age where emergency information is virtually instantaneous, is a 15 minute or longer diatribe by you or other broadcast meteorologists whereby the same information is repeated over and over again. Equally, if not more annoying is your particularly condescending and pedantic style of delivering your report. It's as if you're addressing a 3rd grade elementary school class. (Save that for the school classroom where I know you have presented many times) I, at least, am not an idiot. Maybe your focus groups are comprised of high school dropouts, but most viewers of local news probably are not (I'd bet the vast majority of the viewers have smart phones and a weather app too).

+++

Tornado warning interruption, complaint: As I sat down to watch a new CSI I was so very rudely interrupted by one of your freaking weather updates. There is no reason for this. Those of us who are literate should not be punished for those few who cant read. Please take into consideration that people turn to CBS for the evening programming and not a 15 min interruption of those shows that keep your news on the air. It isn't necessary to break into our programming during regular shows break during commercials. Thanks for getting me COMPLETELY lost and confused. I hope you will be planning to rerun this episode so we can get caught up on what happened.

+++

Tornado warning interruption, complaint: Why did you time your alert to interrupt the beginning of CSI????? You could have come on before the show - or waited 1 minute and come on after the beginning. The beginning of shows like CSI is so crucial. You ruined it for me. You were redundant and also talked about things that weren't important. Get to the point! You could have made your point within 2 minutes and timed it when the commercials were on.

+++

Tornado warning interruption, complaint: I can't believe you interrupted the first CSI show of 2008! You are an IDIOT!!!! It should only take 15 sec to tell everyone that the weather is bad. But, you just go on, and on, and on... Of all of the stations on the air, you take the longest to make a simple point, and we don't want to hear your crap. Next time, interrupt a commercial!

+++

Tornado warning interruption, complaint: I have looked forward to watching CSI all day. Your station ruined the show for me with your interruption at the beginning of the show for a weather alert. I can read anything put across the bottom of the screen just as well & remain a content viewer of your station. This was a tornado warning which I realize is very serious - but who in this part of the country is prepared for a tornado anyway? Regardless, everytime we have a little rain, your station thinks it needs to buzz in on shows to tell us its raining in Jackson, Alabama or Ocean Springs, MS. If I wanted to watch the weather each time it rains, I'll tune in The Weather Channel.

+++

Tornado warning interruption, complaint: Can you please get this f###g idiot of a weather presenter off the television. I'm trying to watch the golf. Yes I get it, we are under a tornado watch. A 2 minute broadcast is turning into a 25 minute and counting one. This pipsqueak has now started to talk about [Tropical Storm] Julian which is of f##k all significance to anybody. Get the loser off the TV. No, I'm not upset at all btw. Just a wee commentary. Even my family visiting from Ireland are laughing at this clown.

Not to mention your weather broadcast is sponsored. Wtf is all that about. Idiots.

They don't hold back

More than 90% of the communications I've gotten from viewers over the years have been positive and complimentary. The other 10% have been mixed, with the smallest percentage being the ones that are most memorable, in a bad or ugly sort of way. Later in my career, these diminished because my demeanor and graying hair calls for respect. For younger broadcasters, particularly women, it is more than disheartening to have people pick on you in ways that would lead to a physical altercation followed by a police report if they did it to a stranger in person. I've left the spellings and misspellings as they were sent to me by email or social media in the comments that follow:

+++

Comment: Will you tell mr.Seales that thursday is Thanksgiving not turkey day. It might be in his religion but not mine .....I'm a 21 year veteran and have a lot t be thankful for.

My thoughts: When did Thanksgiving become a religious or military holiday?

+++

Comment: Why do all the mewcasters on all the channels wear jackets and ties except Mr Seales ?

One year later, same sender, comment: I wish you would proof read you forcast and maps before you go live and find you have error. Also other newscasters wear their jackets when on air - it is more professional.

Two years later, same sender, comment: Why do ALL you male newscaster -EXCEPT ALAN SEALES -all wear a jacket while on the air for a professional appearance. He is the only one who "comes into my house " without a jacket.

My thoughts: I responded to this man several times, but he would not accept my explanation. He also directly contacted my management to complain. For whatever reason, he just wanted to find fault in me.

+++

Comment: Alan Sealls couldn't walk outside and tell whether it is day or night. Yesterday he said the front was coming thru mid-day today. Tonight he says it is coming thru mid-day tomorrow...he is an idiot with all his nursery rimes. This happens every night. Why does he predict weather a week in advance when he can't predict tomorrow's weather.

My response: I appreciate constructive feedback, even from people who don't care for my style, but which one of our newscasts were you watching where I said a cold front was coming through today? I checked our files from the last three days, and I didn't see any place where I said a front was arriving today. Since Monday, I've been consistently talking and showing images with temperatures and cold front having the biggest change for tomorrow morning. On another note, if you reply or contact me in the future, I require the same respect I will give you and any person- don't call me names.

Rebuttal comment: You are correct, I should not have said that and I am sorry I did.

But, you did say the front was coming thru yesterday and then yesterday you sad it was coming thru today. How can you not even know 24 hours in advance what is going to happen and this happens to your forecast regularly. I feel it is more important to you to be cute with your rhyming that to be accurate. I would prefer straight talk as an adult than being talked to like I was in pre-school.

My response: On any given day I do between 9 and 12 individual forecast segments in our newscasts. There's no doubt I could have misspoken and transposed my days of the week in one of them, since weather is unscripted.

Without a doubt, my forecast always was for a front to pass through this morning. We maintain written and video records of our forecasts. I take my forecasting very seriously so if you can tell me which day and which newscast you were watching when you heard me say the front was coming through on Wednesday, that will help me see where I made an error. Keeping in mind that I am forecasting to over 100,000 viewers who live in 13 different counties, if you feel I am regularly making mistakes or not able to accurately forecast weather, please let me know when this happens.

My thoughts: Another person who does not like my style yet can't be specific about what they are complaining about.

+++

Comment: Hey Allen, I notice that you always dress so well, but I must say, the suit you're wearing tonight would be much better off WITHOUT THAT TIE!!! PLEASE!!! You have much prettier ties than that!!! Please do our eyes a favor and leave in the closet where it belongs!!!! I'm sorry, but it does not go with that suite and it's plain, well...........UGLY!!! ---Dawn

+++

Comment: Watching you give the weather is like watching a tennis match. It is very distracting

Race matters

At a business meeting my wife attended, a man learns I am her husband and approaches her with the comment, "He sounds White." He was inebriated. Other people heard the comment and were a little embarrassed. My wife asked him what he meant. He couldn't clearly answer but he implied that because I use the English language well and use words outside of the normal vocabulary of most people, that that is a trait of White people. That's not the case where I come from! All of the Black people and people of multiple ethnicities that I grew up with were articulate, although with a New York accent or an accent of their native country. Whenever I hear that, I always ask, "Do I really speak that well compared to other weathercasters?" I try hard to be grammatically correct and clear in enunciation. I would rate myself higher than the average communicator, but in my line of work, how I present is not unusual. The misperception that it's not ordinary for a Black person to do so is the problem. It also shows that this man doesn't have a diverse set of friends and acquaintances. That misperception also carries to Black people who haven't been exposed to the wide spectrum of Black excellence and achievement that exists.

+++

After I interrupted the program for a tornado warning, a message was left on my phone. "Tell that weatherman to get his black ass off the TV." What does the color of my posterior have to do with how I do my job? Why didn't the caller call me a meteorologist? Perhaps with a superiority complex, he intentionally demoted me from Chief Meteorologist to weatherman.

+++

On my social media account, one day, someone commented, "I wish all Blacks were as classy as Alan Sealls." I couldn't respond with my true thoughts, without hurting someone or starting a fight. My first thought was, "I wish ALL PEOPLE were as classy as I am." My second thought was, "You obviously don't know many Black people. All the ones I know are classy." Those are thoughts I kept to myself.

+++

In a couple of TV weather segments, I showed dramatic video of a fire whirl in Australia and explained the physics behind how they happen. The video clip was posted all over the internet and easy to find. I later posted a clip of a fire whirl from Montana on my Facebook page, to make the point that fire whirls are not as unusual as people might think. The next day on TV I showed a different fire whirl clip that I verbally referenced as from "northern California from the Fish and Wildlife Service." On the screen I had the initials USFWS to credit the source.

Within 5 minutes of the segment, a viewer sent an email to the station saying, "The Black gentelman *(that's how she spelled it)* was wrong" and that the video was from Australia. In all capital letters, she followed up with that if I am going to do something I should get my facts right. I immediately responded in an even tone with the facts as stated above, with an internet link to the video I showed from California. I closed the email with "Thanks for watching." One might think the viewer would respond with an apology but no, there was no response. This lady was so sure she was right, yet she was 100% wrong, and after accusing me of being wrong she could say nothing. Why would she refer to me as the "Black gentelman" rather than as the weather guy? My station had two other Black gentlemen working on-air that day. How is my skin color relevant to whether I am right or wrong?

+++

A lady contacted me to ask, "Why does the media use the Muslim word haboob?" It took me a while to formulate an answer, where I could teach her, without attacking her misguided and backward view. Muslim is not a language. Here's what I wrote: "I can't speak for the rest of the media but here's some background on weather

… The word Haboob has Arabic origins because they are most common in the Middle East region, and also in India. They were documented there many hundreds of years ago so that's why the name sticks. As far as I know, the word has nothing to do with a particular religion. It's one of dozens of words that do not have English or American origins that meteorologists have used for over a century. A lot of weather words come from many centuries ago. Tornado, derecho, and Santa Ana (winds) have Spanish origins. A Chinook wind is named after the Native American tribe. The word smog comes from Europe. All the cloud names have Latin origins. On the other hand, hurricane names are chosen by the World Meteorological Organization to represent names from all the nations they impact."

I never heard back from her.

Celebrity Waiter

My general manager asked me to be a celebrity waiter for a local organization's fundraiser. He said one of the other anchors agreed to help out. I've done those sorts of events before, so it didn't seem to be a problem, except it was on a Sunday and I hate to shave and get dressed for events to give up weekend time. I asked him where it would be, and he told me at the local country club. This was an old-money, old-Mobile, exclusive White man's club, literally up until a decade earlier. I had been to a few events there, and actually had dinner there with one of its first Black members just a couple of months earlier.

I immediately saw the irony in me, a Black man, serving what would likely be a largely White upper-class crowd. I paused, and then with a smile told my GM that I had just seen the movie, "The Butler". That movie told the story of a poor Black child who became a butler at the White House and spent his life serving powerful White people, while trying to maintain his identity and self-worth.

My GM immediately turned red, realizing that having me as a celebrity waiter at that club had an entirely different meaning to a Black person. I laughed even further at his embarrassment because it was genuine, and he never would have thought of the connotations of his request until I had mentioned it. He assured me that if I felt uncomfortable that I should decline but then he admitted that the organization actually had asked for me specifically. I laughed even harder because that could have other meaning, but I did agree to help out. I ended up doing the event, and yes, it was uncomfortable, especially when we volunteers were encouraged by the organization to do silly things to get people to make larger donations. No, I didn't do it again.

Sounding Smart

Upon invitation, I visited a small but fast-growing technology company in Mobile for a tour. The staff were genuinely nice people. One young lady with a strong Southern accent told me where she went to college. As I was about to leave, she sincerely asked, "You sound smart. You're not from here. Where did you go to college?" Her supervisor and I laughed because she didn't realize she verbalized her thoughts that people from this area do not sound intelligent.

Strange encounter

While out to record a short video segment at Mobile's Cathedral Square, my photographer Tim and I are on the steps of a church looking at camera angles and lighting. I note a 30ish man wearing jeans and a military jacket approaching. He saw our news van with the giant station logo and then spotted me. I was hoping he was just going to say hello and keep walking, but I could tell he was determined to get to us. He finally reached us.

"Can your TV station find people?" he asked. I wasn't sure what he wanted or needed but I didn't want to start a long conversation. "Not really any better than the average person," I said. "Well, I'm looking for a guy and I had his email and I emailed him, but he never emailed me back." I figured he was looking for a relative or old friend, so I suggested he try basic web searches using mailing addresses.

"I already tried that, and I got his email, but he didn't email me back and I figured you all would be able to do it better than me." He was probably right but that's not what TV stations do for people. That's what private detectives do for a fee!

Then, he points to his stomach and said, "I've got to get something out of here." Now I'm guessing he needs an operation of some sort but I'm not about to ask. Then without any change in expression or demeanor he says, "I'm looking for an exorcist and the one I found didn't get back to me."

Now, I'm really studying him to see if he is going to smile and let on that he was joking. No smile. I spot some sort of tattoo on his neck, but I don't even try to figure out what it is. I'm keeping my eyes on him, hoping he's not going to pull something out of his shirt that I don't want to see. With my best poker face, I suggest he try the telephone book yellow pages or the reference desk at the library. "They helped me at the library to get the email," he said. "And I'm just trying to get this demon out of me."

He continued for a couple more minutes before turning to leave. "Good luck with it," I said. I'm not sure what "it" was but if he was serious, he needed it. Tim and

I laugh. The irony is we were standing on the steps of a cathedral. It was all I could do to not tell the guy to just go inside and ask for help. It's humorous but also not, as he may well have been dealing with mental illness.

Sailor controls weather

I answered the phone to a man who asked to speak to a meteorologist. I identified myself when I spoke, but he didn't recognize me. That turned out to be a good thing. "I'm a meteorologist," I replied. "I just want to let you know that I'm with the Navy," the man started. He didn't give a rank or title or name, so I immediately was skeptical. He also spoke rapidly with pauses and some stuttering. The man continued, "I'm in charge of a Navy ship and I want to let you know that I'm the one who will let you know what to do when storms are coming." Now, I was convinced this man was not totally balanced. Respectfully, I listened further to see what he really wanted. He asked if I was familiar with a specific Navy ship. I wasn't but I affirmed just to get him closer to the end of his story, although I wasn't really sure if it was really the name of a ship. "Well, when storms are out in the ocean, I'll be letting the media, and Mobile County, know what to do." He seemed to believe what he was saying although he couldn't communicate it well. He said, "Let me know how to contact you with information." There's no way I was going to give him any further access to the weather office! Not knowing how to respond to his fantasy or fabrication, I wanted to get him off the phone quickly, so I politely said, "I appreciate the call. Go ahead and give me your name and number so I can file it." I didn't tell him that I was filing it amongst the many names and phone numbers of callers to avoid. He gave his name (with no title) and paused before remembering his phone number. "Okay," I said, "Thanks." I hoped that that would be his signal to hang up, but it wasn't. He rambled more about bad storms coming and this being the end of times, while he referred to the Book of Revelation. He confirmed my thoughts that he was off balance. In these type calls I try to remain polite and understanding, but when I can tell the person just wants to talk, I give them a little time but that's it. I'm very aware of personality disorders and mental illness and in being in the public eye, I make sure to upset no one who may later come after me.

From time to time, I'll get a communication from someone about a weather conspiracy theory, and sometimes an outright accusation that I am part of the conspiracy or part of a misled group of scientists passing on bad or false information. If I respond, I make it simple, with something like this:

When it comes to what you see on TV, I can't speak for other media outlets but if you are accusing me or any of my weather staff of falsifying information or knowingly exaggerating for the purpose of increasing viewership then that's an attack on professional integrity, not how weather data is gathered. On that charge you are wrong. If I knew of any broadcaster or government meteorologist who purposely put out false information, I would take a stand against them. I've flown with the Hurricane Hunters. I've gone to grad school with NOAA researchers and forecasters, I've been on committees with climatologists. I work closely with our local National Weather Service, and I can tell you in no uncertain terms that these men and women are dedicated to providing the best possible information to the public for protection of life and property.

Moon lady

An older lady called to ask when the next full moon was. I pulled out an almanac and gave her the answer. I figured that was the end of the call but then she asked for the full moon after that one, and then the next one, and then the next. Since I had the almanac in front of me those were easy replies. I was about to hang up and she asked, "Don't you want to know why I'm asking?" I really didn't, since I was in the middle of other tasks. She went on to say, "If you cut your grass when the moon is full it won't grow as fast." That was the first time I'd ever heard that. I almost wanted to ask if she meant cut it at night in the light of the moon, but I didn't want to go any further with that myth. In my mind, I'm envisioning someone in their birthday suit, under a full moon, cutting the grass. Some things you can't convince people of and fortunately this

247

myth is harmless, unless you do get out in the middle of the night and wake up your neighbors with a lawn mower!

+++

Comment: I used to love to watch your forecasts, because it seemed you just loved weather. Does it hurt your heart to stand there now and spew the script? "barrels of buttery sunshine and sapphire skkes" while the planes spray poison until the sun is a hazy blob in a poisoned sky? While you fumble with phrases like "rare reflective cloud rainbow" or "bomb cyclone". I was especially impressed with the explanation of the high and low pressure combining to make the u-turn shaped chem trail some photographed last week. I watched it come out of the back of an airplane. Now, you can try to explain I'm crazy, and a conspiracy theorist or whatever. But we know. I just hope you dont forget the truth, and that you think you have a better reason than money for your lies. They are poisoning us, you, and your children and future generations, and you are helping them. I'm sorry for and will pray for you.

My thoughts: I never respond to people with conspiracy theories who accuse me of something I did not do.

+++

Comment: I have two questions regarding the weather daily reports. 1) Is the radar being read by a news forecaster? I ask because it seems like the forecasters are looking at New Orleans to see what's going on there and attempting to predict the weather for Mobile. If it's raining in NO that doesn't mean it's going to rain here! Mississippi is between LA and AL or did you guys forget that? 2) Why does our weather forecast stem from what is going on in New Orleans? I have family and friends there and most of the time y'all say it's raining there, it's not. That info is just a phone call away. To put it bluntly, y'all look like you don't know what the heck you're doing! Do you?

My response: Thanks for the feedback on our weather broadcasts. I'm trying to get a better idea of when you say most of the time when we say it's raining in New Orleans that it's not. Is this something that has been going on for days, months, or years? Is it a specific weather forecaster? Can you give me any specific dates? I can tell you that New Orleans is a large enough city that it rarely rains in the entire city at one time so any given neighborhood may not be getting wet. Our local forecasts are not based on N.O. weather. It is though, one factor, when the steering flow is west to east.

Rebuttal comment: Mr. Seals, I do not have specific dates, but I do listen to you at 10:00 o'clock every night and you have made some of those mistakes to. I know that New Orleans is a large City, I just recently moved from there to here. I have friends and relatives all over the city and I call randomly to see if it's raining there when it is forecasted here. After living there 15 years, you would think this is something I can find out about. Saturday was the last day, I can think of off bat, but it's usually a weekly thing. But your station isn't the only station in Mobile who does this. Now, tell me that wasn't you on television last season with all those depressions/hurricanes that didn't pan out? Shall I name them? I listened then, just as I listen now and it's not the best weather report in the World. All I'm saying is you guys need to rethink what you're doing, although it doesn't seem to bother the locals who have been here forever. Correct it! Don't write back! I will be watching to see the weather report and to see what improvements you have made.

My response #2: I must reply when you tell me to correct a forecast. What you call a mistake in a forecast implies that something that can be measured is interpreted wrong. By definition a forecast is a prediction of the future, not a guarantee. I'm still not clear if you are saying that we say it is raining in N.O. and it is not, or we say it will rain in N.O. and it doesn't or if you are talking about our forecast for the Mobile area. I also don't understand what you mean by depressions/hurricanes that did not pan out. I can tell you with 100% certainty that I never said any tropical system was going to strike us last year. I put a lot of effort in delivering a comprehensive forecast and if it falls short in any way or definition, I honestly appreciate note of a specific incident. Is your perspective that all Mobile TV station forecasts are not good enough, not as good as New Orleans TV stations forecasts, or something other?

Rebuttal again comment: We can go back and forth with this indefinitely, but I refuse to. The weatherman always show a forecast that it's raining in New Orleans and add "we should expect rain here in a couple of hours" or "we should be getting some of that rain here." The hurricanes & depressions were predicted last season and each time a heavy rain was sighted in the Atlantic or the Gulf it was broadcasted over the waves. Half of the depressions were just rains in the Gulf and Atlantic Ocean. It does rain in the ocean and in the gulf or does no one consider that factor. For you. I do not have to compare New Orleans with Mobile because there are no comparisons! You can talk until you're blue in the face but it doesn't change what's being said on tv. I DO know the difference between a forecast and a prediction, but when the weather people (here) began getting upset or reporting false details I question it. Now that we have gotten this out of the way, have a good day.

My thoughts: This lady just wanted to ramble and complain about something but I'm not even sure if it was directed at me!

+++

Comment: I can't believe you actually buy into the hype. Weather goes in a cycle. I remember in the 70's when the alarmists were don't use aerosol cans -we are going to have another ice age now it is global warming. GET REAL. God has this in control. But bth there weill be global warming in the tribulation... God is going to scorch this earth weih heat like you haven't ever experienced but there isn't a thing you can do about it except make sure to get saved before Jesus comes and miss the tribulation! This nonsense on global warming is just like the obama helathcare it is all about CONTROL!

+++

Comment: A very close friend of mine and myself were looking at the terrible storms that were coming from the midwest to the eastern USA on the days recently past. We were amazed at the power and strong red lines of severe weather being registered on weather doppler radar seen on websites online... I noticed with some surprise the obvious sign of 3 ufos in a perfectly uniform formation off the coast of the Carolinas and I quickly went on the other sites I use to file a copy of the photo image... my friend was able to secure a single still photo (8:17 PM) showing the ufos and at my end on a different computer I was able to secure the original photo (7:23 PM) showing what was going on about 40 minutes before the ufos appeared off the coast over the Atlantic Ocean. My guess was they were about 200 miles offshore... I became increasingly concerned when I suddenly saw an obvious pattern in the red zones showing up of severe weather beginning over some southern USA states 40 minutes earlier before the ufos showed up off the coast...Had they been in a state of hover over the states earlier where the severe storm patterns showed up ? The angle of the 3 storm zones and distance apart was exactly the same as the formation the ufos had 40 minutes later nearby. I decided to go public with the info just to be sure that if the type of severe weather seen did not go away in the months ahead, at least I would know I had tried to raise an alert, a warning about something odd, something awesomely terrifying if it were ever proven to be true. The use of weather as a weapon . I hope I am wrong.

My thoughts: I hope you are wrong too.

+++

Comment: Stop exaggerating the wind speed. With Katrina and Ivan, I tracked them across the Gulf and while all TV wx people were reporting 135 mph winds, the highest sustained winds was 70 mph with only one gust to 90 mph. Why not use data buoy winds? Using other sources implies that you are attempting to obfuscate (blow smoke up the viewing public's skirts) so they will stay glued to your station. The same goes for all the t/s warnings that never amount to much, especially if you've lived here a long time, i.e. 70+ years! This type of reporting appears to have started in the late 90s with all the new carpetbaggers arriving and the advent of all the new gee whiz electronics!

My thoughts: I went back and forth with this man for a few years trying to get him to understand that the highest wind in a hurricane cannot be recorded. It is estimated by extrapolation, pressure, satellite, and other data. He never accepted that.

Good comments

The positive words from people, and the questions and comments from kids, make the job fun. At a school visit in the early 2000s, a time when every home still had a paper phone book with emergency evacuation routes and maps listed, I quizzed the children, "Name a book that everyone has, but no one uses anymore, that has hurricane safety information." One kid responded, "A dictionary!" Another kid answered, "The Bible!" The teachers and I had a good laugh.

Here are more random comments I've received that gave me a smile:

+++

Just wanted to express our thanks for the great weather reports you give us each day when you are on the air. I have been traveling the US & Canada for over 30 years and watched reports from stations from everywhere on the continent, and you are the best!

+++

Your broadcasts during Katrina and its aftermath have been a lifesaver, literally. Many of us used the information you provided to prepare for our safety and well-being. Your professionalism is outstanding. Thank you again.

+++

Every hurricane that we get through brings our family even closer to you. You are a true professional and we sincerely appreciate how you know how to report on hurricanes without being alarming. We love you. Keep up the good work and God Bless. – Dianne

+++

Alan you are the best. You were so nice to me when we met after my daughter was killed and I'm a forever fan

+++

I am a young 70 year old woman, and I just want to say that you really impress me. You remind me of an impish little boy, but you really know your stuff. Keep up the good work. – Mary

+++

I love to listen to your presentation of the weather because you are understandable. As a teacher, I appreciate the educational information you give about the weather and when I was teaching the "weather" part of earth science I would ask my students to listen to your broadcast. You seem to have a wonderful personality and brighten my day as I watch you and the rest of the team. Thank you.

+++

When you first came to Mobile I wasn't sure I'd be able to watch your forcasts. Frankly, it was a color problem. I really didn't care for the purple suit. ☺ Now years later you could deliver the weather in a clown suit and I'd not notice. Yours is the weather of choice for me. I like your presentation, your manner and the person-to-person style. You're first rate and my worry is that the really big markets are going to find out about you. Best regards and a Merry Christmas to you and your family. – Wallace

+++

His voice is low and soft, a piece of silk you might keep in a drawer and pull out only on rare occasions, just to feel it between your fingers.

Alan Sealls

CHAPTER 11

Tornado Emergency

The forecast routine of a broadcast meteorologist overwhelmingly involves benign weather conditions. Those are the days when we should be preparing for the inevitable dangerous or violent weather scenarios. It's not hard for a person with personality to be a sunny-day forecaster, where they can make light of calm weather, or have a tiny error in the forecast that has little impact on the public.

Friday, April 15, 2011, was a day that was not so calm in my Mobile, Alabama, broadcast area. This was a day projected by computer models to deliver severe weather. To a meteorologist, it was a classic spring storm with the center moving out of the Plains, eastward across the Ohio valley. My region first would get a warm front in the morning, preceding a warm sector of air, followed by a cold front late in the evening. I expected it to be a routine day of covering severe weather, but it was not. People died.

I managed to get a full night's sleep beforehand and that turned out to be valuable. Upon waking at 10 am, everything I looked at showed an atmosphere primed for severe storms. In fact, a tornado watch was issued, with Mobile County in the southeastern corner of the watch. Usually that means we have hours until the storms arrive from the west; but since a warm front was moving northward, within minutes, severe storms formed immediately to our west and tracked northeastward through a few of our inland, low population counties. Before 11 am, the first tornado warning was issued. I turned on the TV to my station to see the radar during the program interruption. I was happy to see there were just a few thunderstorm cells, but I was surprised to see a couple of them had radar signatures of mini-supercells. A supercell is a thunderstorm with persistent broad rotation, and a strong updraft. On the northern Gulf of Mexico coast, we often get smaller versions of supercells, known as mini-supercells, but they are still a threat. Typically, these would move north with the warm front and exit our area, but not today. Another warning shortly followed, and I could see that these discrete storms were going to be a problem, so I started preparing to go to work, 3 hours early. Shortly after I showered and dressed, the station called. I knew why. "I'm on the way," I announced. I grabbed a plastic bag and filled it with leftovers, and then set my DVR to record my station the whole day. That was to later review my performance and our coverage.

I arrived at work by 11:30 am and my morning forecaster was still on the air with cut-ins. I immediately went into the routine that had become routine, especially that year. We had already had an extended severe weather outbreak with several EF2 tornadoes in the heart of our viewing area five weeks earlier. Following that, I had further prepared severe weather routines and duties for the weather team. I coordinated with the newsroom and set up my graphics on our computers. The phones were ringing with a handful of viewer complaints for interrupting their programs. That's expected. Just two weeks earlier, during the final game of the NCAA championship, the phones really rang as I had to interrupt games several times with tornado warnings. Fortunately, there were no tornadoes. As disconcerting as complaints are, I remind myself that a few dozen complaints, from irate, rude, and repeat callers experiencing "remote rage" is nothing when there are over 100,000 people watching.

Within a few minutes I was on-air, giving my morning forecaster a chance to breathe. We continued for an hour, working as a tag team, through our noon newscast. Continuous broadcast coverage of severe weather is often called "wall to wall," because we cover over all programming the way a carpet covers an entire floor, from wall to wall. Pictures began to come in of funnel clouds and hail, followed by reports of a few homes destroyed and damaged in one of our inland counties. Several people were injured and taken to the hospital. The radar showed the cells following the same paths in our inland counties and maintaining a textbook signature of hooks. There was no end in sight. We had live reports from the damage area which gave us meteorologists a break in continuous talking. I took the opportunity to scarf down some food. My energy was falling since I had not eaten breakfast. As bad luck would have it, I had just finished stuffing chicken in my mouth when the anchor tossed back to me. Even though I had swallowed it, I had a hard time talking for about 3 minutes. It was a challenge.

Through 3 pm, another round of mini-supercells traversed the same inland area, forcing us to continue program interruptions for most of that period. There was a lull between 3 pm and 7 pm when the morning forecaster got to go home. I continued shorter cut-ins, several times an hour. I was able to prepare my forecast and normal broadcast graphics. As is always the case in this type of weather, I could only keep up. I had no time to analyze data or even save important graphic snapshots of the event. The best I could do was watch the satellite and radar and trends, but in a case like this, with experience, that's all that needs to be done. Rarely is it a question of what will happen later or tomorrow. In severe weather, the number one concern is what is happening now and who is in danger. Following that, is the question of where the danger is going to be in the immediate future.

Through afternoon, as we were entirely in the warm air sector, the storms continued in the same inland counties. This was surprising, but I could only guess that outflow from thunderstorms had created a boundary to serve as the focus for new storms. Farther west, across the Mississippi River, I kept looking for a squall line to form, but none ever congealed. There were a few supercells there, but only as a semi-broken line. My fear was that in the heat of the afternoon we might have explosive development locally, but again, I had no time to analyze whether this was likely.

Even though our afternoon programs were very popular, I did not get one complaint after noon through the rest of what would become nearly 14 hours of weather coverage, with a total program interruption time of nearly 5 hours. The complaints stop when even the most callous person sees that the danger of the weather actually is more important than what's regularly on TV.

Just after 7 pm, the sun set but the storms did not let up. Tornado warnings were again issued in the same inland counties. Now that we were in prime-time programming, I made the decision to try to do updates only in commercial breaks, and only over national commercials, not local commercials. Without running local commercials, we lose revenue.

Radar signatures were still discrete supercells, and larger than the cells earlier in the day. My morning forecaster returned shortly after 7 pm for backup as he saw activity picking up. Unfortunately, our weekend meteorologist was out of town. It's critical to have 3 or more sets of eyes and hands in extended coverage, but the financial nature of television broadcasting had forced us too often to do it with only 2.

Around 8 pm things got worse. At this point, 10 hours after the first warnings, the thunderstorm cells were still tracking in the same 3 inland counties and only slowly sagging south toward Mobile.

A tornado emergency was issued by the National Weather Service. From past weather conferences, I knew what that meant. There was a large tornado with extreme likelihood of injury and death. I had never uttered that phrase in my career, so this was a first for me and for Mobile. I stayed on the air for over 30 minutes with my morning forecaster backing me up. As before, I did not have time to fully digest the rationale for that particular emergency, but the radar signature was obviously showing a strong and large hook rotation.

It was around this same time that I realized that the radar data had stopped updating. I had been distracted by switching to alternate data, so I missed the formation of this threat. It wasn't until the next day when I accompanied the National Weather Service on a damage survey that I was reminded that what I saw on radar was a debris ball signature—a pattern where radar can detect a ball of lofted objects that are not rain or hail. It was painfully obvious the next day, but in the heat of the coverage, my mind had never expected to see that. It's one of the things you learn and read about but if you're not looking for it, it can sneak by. This is why after each major event it's critical to go back to the radar archives and run through them.

Right after the tornado emergency, it took a while for my station and for me to hear of the outcome. We started getting reports of people in three communities being injured and missing. We also got reports of one community being destroyed. The news department put in great effort to confirm these, but given that it was after dark, power was lost, roads were blocked, and these were small or rural communities that were hit, it took a long time to get credible confirmation. Many of the calls or emails were based on word-of-mouth reports that often were exaggerated or skewed by emotion. On this night the reports turned out to be true.

Over the next three hours we found that three people had been killed in two different communities. All of them were in mobile homes that were destroyed. This was the day I had mentally prepared for. I had no time to be sad or emotional. I could only say a little prayer and keep going.

The tornado threat and cut-ins continued until past midnight. In our 10 pm news, even though we had the reports, we had no pictures of the new damage or fatality areas. That made it difficult for me and for everyone to grasp. By midnight, the extent of the damage was confirmed, but we still had no pictures. Our crews could not physically get to the impact areas. Finally, by 1 am, the tornado threat diminished and ended as the broken squall line ahead of the cold front moved through. My morning guy left, and I stayed until 2:30 am.

I had gotten an email from the Mobile National Weather Service that they would be doing a damage survey at 8 am. As tired as I was, I had to go. I had never seen the process and I needed to know what actually happened so that I could compare it to what I saw on radar and learn from it. With only a few hours of sleep, I followed them to the hardest hit areas of Leakesville, Mississippi, and Burbank, Alabama.

The damage was about what I expected, having seen other tornado and hurricane damage. In one of the small communities that viewers had said was "demolished" and "wiped off the map," the truth was half the community took the direct impact of an EF3 tornado while the other half was not hit. However, the level of destruction in the path was high.

On a sunny, dry, cool morning, just 12 hours after the tornado went through, a couple of things amazed me. Number one was how many people recognized me and were happy to see a "TV celebrity." Some of the survivors whose homes were destroyed greeted me with smiles. One man asked for an autograph and many people stopped to shake my hand. As odd as it seemed, I was glad that just being there gave people a reason to smile.

Many of the survivors were still in what I call functional shock and surprise that they were hit. By that I mean they were going about the cleanup process mechanically, and able to hold a conversation. All of them wanted to talk and tell their story, even though I was not interviewing them with a microphone. I was happy to hear that each person said they took shelter, although it was literally at the last second. Their families and neighbors were all milling around giving support emotionally and physically. Every single person was positive and optimistic. It was clear that they valued life over property. In fact, in one home, next to mobile homes in which people were killed, during the cleanup someone tossed a bunch of women's clothes out of a closet. The husband looked at the wife and said, "Where'd those come from?" She said they were hidden way back in the closet. He laughed, and so did everyone else. A typical marital exchange at the scene of a near-disaster.

In each of the impact areas, the damage patterns were typical of tornadoes as a narrow path of missing roofs, severely damaged homes, uprooted and snapped trees, and overturned vehicles. All of the clichés you've ever heard about tornado damage were seen.

I was amazed that more people did not die. Dozens of homes had 1 or 2 walls collapsed. Mobile homes were overturned and demolished. Watching the damage survey was fascinating. In some cases, it was easy to see how wide the tornado was, based on the debris pattern and how the trees were blown down. In other cases, it was impossible for me to determine, but after listening to the survey team's descriptions things began to make sense. I was impressed at the diligence the National Weather Service survey team exercised but also at the sensitivity and compassion they showed in dealing with people who had just lost property, and in some cases loved ones. I could see they did not want to intrude, but for the sake of understanding what happened they almost had to.

As meteorologists, they took it personally that people had lost their lives, and their mission was to do everything possible to ensure it wouldn't happen again. I share that goal, as a broadcast meteorologist, but that's an impossible task given mobile homes, building codes, communications, our ability to detect storm hazards, and human nature in reacting to threats. We can only hope that everyone learns from these disasters so that there is less damage, injury, and death in the future.

CHAPTER 12

Oil and Weather do Mix

April 20, 2010, the British Petroleum Deepwater Horizon oil rig explosion in the northern Gulf of Mexico kills eleven people. The oil rig was about 100 miles south of Mobile Bay and the Alabama coast, and about 45 miles southeast of the mouth of the Mississippi River in southeastern Louisiana. According to NOAA, there are more than 3,800 oil and gas rigs in the Gulf, so an explosion is not unheard of; however, this one was different in that the entire oil rig caught on fire and then tumbled into the water. At this location, the water depth is about 5,000 feet.

I was on vacation from my TV job as chief meteorologist at the CBS TV station in Mobile, but I was in town. I was busy around the house with projects, so I did not watch much news. I knew of the explosion but didn't give it much thought, even after the rig went into the water. Initial reports from BP were that some oil was leaking, but even that didn't seem too much of a problem, separated from the loss of life that had occurred. That changed quickly.

Within a few days, it became clear that oil had not just spilled, it was leaking, but not like a leak from a ship with a fixed amount of oil. This was a leak from a pipe near the seafloor. The source of oil had no limit. Within a month, the disaster created the largest oil spill in U.S. history. More correctly, it was a leak. BP attempted various methods to stop the leak, slow it, and then finally siphon it. After two months they made some progress, but without complete success. At whatever point the leak would totally stop would be too late for the beaches and marshes of Louisiana, Alabama, and the Florida Panhandle. Oil was moving and spreading.

Once the scope of the potential environmental disaster became clear, just a few days after the explosion, TV meteorologists were called into action as "station scientists" to cover a topic that none of us had considered or prepared for. We were expected to deliver daily perspective, satellite views and forecasts of the oil leak, while instantly becoming hydrologists, geologists, oceanographers, and marine scientists. Resources and data were scarce and not routinely available.

I was called in to work extra days and hours, as my weekend meteorologist was put on duty as a reporter. As our understanding of the event grew by the second weekend after the explosion, we had our primary news anchor team on-air, as we would for any major news event. My TV station quickly set up a special section on our website. One feature was a twice-daily update from the weather team on what the oil was doing. As the story unfolded, we ended up with record visits to our website, far exceeding those from during and after Hurricane Katrina.

Initial attempts to know and explain what was happening were difficult due to lack of timely official information. There was no available routine daily estimate of the boundaries and motion of the oil. Trajectory forecasts by NOAA were helpful, but not necessarily accurate. Estimates of the oil leaking were suspected to be too low. Every few weeks, estimates were raised while many oceanographers and marine specialists still felt they were far too low.

As a news department, we looked for a variety of sources of information. I feared that we might be giving a little too much credibility to certain websites and professors that sounded good but maybe had an agenda to promote. News anchors and meteorologists broadcast assumptions about what was happening and what was expected to happen early on in the disaster. In some cases, we drew parallels to tropical storm predictions and motions which turned out to be misleading, if not wrong.

Based on the principle that oil and water don't mix, and that oil floats on water, I developed in my mind the picture of oil rising straight from the ocean floor and then spreading out on the surface. I assumed thick oil would hold together in a mass with little or no evaporation. I was wrong.

I came to learn that crude oil has varying density. Some of it does float to the surface of the water where it exists as streaks and sheen, but the heavier oil does not immediately float to the top. The ocean is like the atmosphere where there are layers, some stratified and others with more vertical mixing. Combine that with oil of differing density and you get layers of oil in the ocean just like the layers of clouds we find in the atmosphere.

The never-ending difficulty in this situation was that we can see clouds in layers in the atmosphere, but we cannot effectively see and measure clouds and plumes of oil in deep water. Based on available data and images, I could only talk about oil on the surface. That is what we media showed until we were able to get subsurface images and videos from researchers and oceanographers. It was entirely possible, and likely, in my opinion, that the amount of oil beneath the surface far exceeded what we saw on the water. Nonetheless, the only available mapping and forecasts of the oil were just for surface.

Perhaps this played into public and local government perception that the best defense was to set up oil boom containment systems. These are floating barriers that can block surface oil, but the barriers do not extend downward more than a couple of feet. Parts of Louisiana were first to have oil reach the marshes in thick layers, beyond the booms. This could only be possible if subsurface oil were to move toward the coast, underneath the booms, and then ascend or follow the slope of the underwater terrain to the surface.

Much of what I learned in the first month of the oil leak was from observation followed by deduction. I did make another poor assumption early on and that was that the oil would primarily be moved by wind. Our region's prevailing warm season wind is from the south or southeast, due to the Bermuda High. We thought the wind would rapidly push the oil toward us. Day after day we watched as my weather team and I incorporated wind information in our discussions. After about two weeks, we noticed that the entire spill area was not moving toward us, it was actually moving more to the west, approaching the southern Louisiana coast. We hoped that the leak could be stopped before anything would change this trend. After several weeks, there still was no oil close to the Alabama coast and the size of the surface oil had not really grown much, even though many experts estimated the leak rate was large and even increasing.

That's when I deduced that a couple of things were occurring. The first was that the oil was being controlled more by ocean currents than by wind. Wind can push ships and sailboats since both have large components sitting above the water. Oil is on the water's surface but really is in the water's surface. After doing a little research, I found a typical water current in the northern Gulf is about 1 mph. If the direction changes a bit every few days, that could account for oil not moving toward us, even if the wind is blowing toward us.

I then followed an internet link to *Oil in the Sea III*, a book compiled by the National Research Council's Committee on Oil in the Sea. This book covers many aspects of oil production. I did not read the entire book but glanced over several chapters. The statistic that stood out to me was that 10% of heavy surface crude oil can evaporate within a few days, while 40% of medium crude does so, and up to 75% of light crude does so as well.

The evaporation rate, combined with ocean currents gave me further hope that the oil would never reach our shoreline. I was not alone.

Gradually, daily projections from NOAA put the threat of oil in my area in the middle of May. For days, no oil was sighted but we did begin to smell what later turned out to be oil in the Gulf. The odor was like burning diesel fuel. It was no stronger than what you would notice sitting in heavy traffic, but it was noticeable. I realized that to understand this I had to see for myself what was happening. One month after the spill, I went to Dauphin Island, Alabama, on my day off, to see the National Guard erecting Hesco-brand barriers in a chain around the entire residential barrier island. Hesco barriers are sand-filled cages that are used in warfare to protect fighters from bullets and shrapnel.

I also observed the boom containment systems in the water. My first thought was, "If the boom stops the oil, how is it all then disposed of safely?" My second thought, as I looked offshore at a natural gas rig just a few miles away from a marina was, "How can we not live without oil and gas energy and is there any energy that is truly safe to gather?"

Mobile, Alabama, was one of the government Unified Command Response centers. We have a major U.S. Coast Guard Base, so this gave me the unique opportunity in the fifth week to fly as a media observer on a U.S. Coast Guard C-144. It's a smaller version of the Hurricane Hunter C-130, also with a rear cargo bay and a limited number of small windows.

My flight was enlightening, personally and professionally. At the time, there was no oil near the Alabama or Florida shore. Even though the small windows prevented a true panoramic view, and even though I was busy taking video and still photo images, I could see it was real. We in TV often don't connect with the images on the screen because it's simply TV. But once you are there, there's no question. This was immense. It was still hard to believe that this disaster had occurred and was ongoing.

We flew at 500 feet above the Gulf of Mexico. Given the speed of the plane and my mission to capture images, it was difficult to really analyze the oil. The first thing that struck me was that the oil was never solid. There were widespread areas of sheen, but the rust-colored oil was in bands and streaks. It was on the surface and also just beneath the surface. I believe that is why the wind was not so much a factor in motion.

After my flight, I re-examined the graphic we used on TV to show projections, which was composed of a semi-transparent yellow polygon, with darker orange spots representing heavy oil. I made a template using a rust-colored semi-transparent blob with breaks in the color. It actually looked like what I saw from the air. I had my weather team vote on it. One person liked the old way to maintain consistency and the other person felt it was too scary. My response at that time was, "You mean it's not scary?!" This was weeks before the rust-colored oil started showing up on our beaches. It was scary.

As a team, we did a pretty good job of explaining our graphic, along with the unknowns, so I did not change it. I removed the darker colors for thick oil since those stayed right around the spill source. They were not relevant to our viewers. At least two of our local competitors were using solid dark or bright color polygons which I felt overdid the situation.

Around this same time, our webmaster had been finding many internet websites with model projections and got approval for us to use them on-air. I immediately cautioned him and the news department that no one model had been consistently "accurate," and to show models projecting different scenarios could do more harm than good. It is similar to showing the average person a lot of model track forecasts for hurricanes.

Most of the websites with oil models were from university researchers and most of the displays had surface wind vectors superimposed on the oil. Even though I'm sure the model physics put more weight on the water currents than on the wind, the displays would confuse the average person. Many of the displays also had color tables that were either too ominous or just confusing as to what the colors meant. There was one site in particular which had a model and the word "NEW" right next to it. That's not something I wanted to put my faith in. Fortunately, my news department followed my advice on this.

Aside from delivering daily internet updates, we forecasters were pushed forward as science experts. In most broadcasts we were expected to give information to put the oil in perspective and inform the viewers. Early on in the process, that information consisted mainly of saying where the oil was and converting things like barrels of oil to gallons of oil. I took that a step further to convert it to tanker truckloads of oil, since that's something people can relate to.

We talked daily about uncertainties and unknowns. We later included offshore wind and wave forecasts to give a sense as to whether cleanup mitigation attempts could occur. That was followed by air quality data. I tried to make the analogy that the odor of oil was similar to sitting in traffic by talking about how much gas the average driver burns in a day and a year. One viewer called and accused me of making a political statement on global warming!

As we moved through the end of May and seasonal hurricane forecasts came out for an above-normal season, questions started coming from the viewers of what would happen if a hurricane got in the Gulf. There was national speculation that oil might lessen evaporation and reduce a hurricane threat but locally the fear was more of what would storm surge do to oil and might oil fall in the rain. I began to address these questions every other day.

It was helpful that NOAA put out a "fact sheet" on various scenarios of a hurricane and the oil spill. I made that a permanent part of our website, even though one viewer emailed that I was passing on government propaganda and I didn't check my facts. I responded, detailing my background and experience and the fact that the article was clearly attributed to NOAA. I also reminded him that when NOAA issues Watches and Warnings there's no question as to the motivation of NOAA. Since this was an article of speculation based on solid science, I would have written it the same way. He never responded!

By week 7, I got the sense from family and friends elsewhere in the country that national media was maybe broad brushing what was happening, not intentionally, but more by lack of local detail. There actually was one wrong Associated Press report of ankle-deep oil near a restaurant on one of our beaches. The restaurant owner immediately called us after we broadcast that and said it was not true.

My brother in Washington DC said he didn't want to bring his young sons to visit me that summer because of the air quality in Mobile. I told him that it was actually healthier than the air where he lives but he didn't want to take a chance. Some days the oil odor was immediately noticeable outside but on most days it was subtle. After being outside for a while you wouldn't even notice.

Other friends asked about the oil after seeing images of birds in oil from Louisiana, more than 100 miles away.

The Mobile television market serves an area where the overwhelming majority of the viewers live within 50 miles of the coast. For most of us, the oil threat was not something visual, but it was there. By the second week of June, oil was on our beaches and in some of the marshes. It had a huge negative impact on our tourism and fishing industries. While some tourists cancelled plans to visit to avoid a hazard, I suspect others cancelled based on unknowns, and also in part because I believe the average person is not strong in geography and lumps our entire region together.

Two months after the explosion, my station continued to devote the majority of our news time and resources to the oil, both on-air and on our website. Viewers regularly emailed daily photos of the oil, suggestions on how to stop the leak, and questions on how they can get to the right person or agency to get their lives back in order. I received one direct question from a viewer each week, usually a "what if ..." type question regarding oil and hurricanes, oil and air quality, and oil and lightning. Everyone suddenly became more environmentally aware.

The event was incredible, but not in a positive way. Even now, it's hard to grasp the magnitude of the impact the oil had on our food chain, sea life, the beauty of our coastline, and the local and regional economy. It was like a slow-motion hurricane that takes forever to arrive, and then lingers for an unknown period where you can't begin to plan recovery until all the damage is done. The impact of the oil spill is years, and maybe even multiple decades. It was like a bad horror movie where a monster is on the loose. Unbelievable, bizarre, surreal, and depressing are words that described what was happening. Each day I watched our Coast Guard flying missions to assess and attack the enemy. I learned to identify a Blackhawk helicopter by sound as well as a C-144 airplane. I viewed the large number of out-of-state contractors and coordinators filling our downtown hotels, heading to the coast.

My first trip to the beach after the oil showed up was two months into the leak. This was about three weeks after the oil arrived in layers at Gulf Shores, Alabama. On July 3rd, a sunny, summer afternoon, I arrived at the public beach. The parking lot was full. People were on the sand. Music played in the distance from a restaurant band. Things seemed normal. Even with the satellite truck from CNN parked nearby, it could have been a regular day except the number of people at the beach was probably 20% of what you would expect on a holiday weekend.

The sand looked fine from the parking lot, even with the tracks and trails of heavy machinery that had traveled the length of the beach. I walked toward the surf in the dazzling daylight. Just past the parking lot, tractors were busy grading the sand in the middle of the beach in a long stretch easily of a mile. Most of the beachgoers were at the edge of the sand at the water, but something else was there—a four-foot-high berm. The berm was constructed of sand, piled up to prevent oil from making it far onto the beach. Either it was built too late, or it didn't work. Halfway from the parking lot to the berm, I began to see small specks of semi-solid oil. Most of it was tiny, smaller than confetti. If I were not looking for it, I wouldn't have noticed anything unusual. But then, closer to the water I noticed more and more oil pieces, more the size of lima beans, with other pieces as large as prunes. It was all mixed in with the sand, so some were brown and hard while others were like thick chocolate syrup patties.

Picking it up, I could smell the odor of petroleum, and after a few moments in my hand it left a brown oil residue. People didn't seem to mind walking barefoot on it, but I did. I kept my shoes on. Some tourists were even scooping it up and molding it into balls. It was scattered and mixed in everywhere and not just on the surface of the sand. With my foot, I scraped sand away to a depth of half a foot and the oil was still there in pieces and swirls. Some was hardened but most was like thick molasses. I drove one mile eastward to the other end of the beach, closer to Gulf State Park Pier. The situation there was worse. In this lesser-used part of the beach there were areas that looked like broken blacktop on a parking lot, except what looked like chunks of pavement was sheets of dried oil.

Every few hundred yards, there were work crews of 3 or 4 people wearing boots and gloves raking, sifting, and shoveling oil-soaked sand into plastic bags placed in buckets. The partially-filled bags were then piled up in cordoned-off areas. Cosmetically, the cleaning made a difference, but in my estimation, 10 to 20 times the number of crews would have been needed to have an impact. I thought that there must be some sort of machinery that could sift sand better on a large scale, but cleaning by hand was more environmentally friendly. I do know that hand cleaning employs more individuals and makes it appear that work is being done.

At the surf line near the newly rebuilt Gulf State Park Pier, the stain of oil stayed in the sand, even as wave after wave of water passed over it. I came to the realization that the oil floating on water to be deposited on the sand can't be the only way the beach sand is being contaminated. Oil must be seeping into the sand and moving beneath the beach too. That would explain why digging in the sand turns up more flakes, specks, pieces, and stains of oil.

At the same time, the winds and changing tide levels acted together to create layers of oil and sand that constantly changed. Even if all of the sand had been removed down to the water line, and replaced with new sand from somewhere else, there would have still been the likelihood that new oil from the leak would return or that old oil that was submerged would make it back to the beach.

The situation seemed hopeless and numbing.

Finally, on Thursday, July 15, 2010, after many failed attempts over three months, BP capped the leak. It held. For the first time, things began to look brighter.

The next week brought a major scare. On July 23rd, Tropical Depression 3 formed over the southern Bahamas and then moved into the Gulf of Mexico as minimal Tropical Storm Bonnie. The forecast track projected it almost directly over the oil leak site. Work at the spill site was put on hold. Tropical Storm Bonnie never strengthened much and then weakened to a tropical depression over the spill area before totally fading on Saturday, July 24th.

Through early August, the surface oil was less and less but still sporadic. It became very difficult to say anything specific about it, so we stopped including a weather/oil forecast in every newscast and eventually only mentioned it when there was something noteworthy. Toward middle August, the oil drift was more to the west and southwest, with smaller areas being detected.

On August 10th, Tropical Depression 5 formed in the Gulf of Mexico, west of Fort Myers, Florida. It also had a projection toward southeast Louisiana, taking it over the spill site. Once again, we began the speculation of what wind, waves and surge might do with lingering oil, and subsurface oil. Fortunately, Tropical Depression 5 never strengthened. It dissipated in the north central Gulf of Mexico the next day.

Finally, August 23rd, the final Trajectory Map was issued by NOAA, and we stopped posting streaming video weather updates to our website.

The lessons to broadcast meteorologists, from the oil spill, are that we must have a broad knowledge of general science, not make assumptions, and be able to research and synthesize data and concepts.

CHAPTER 13

What's in the Sky?

E very so often, somebody sends me a video of a bright light in the nighttime sky, and they want to know what it is. They are wise enough to not rely on the University of Social Media for a reasonable answer. I try to investigate if I know where and what time they recorded the video, and which direction they were looking. Most people forget to share those key clues!

To determine what you see in the night sky, get an astronomy app that you hold up to the sky to identify all celestial bodies in their actual positions. Then, get a satellite tracking app. I'm a meteorologist, not an astronomer. Astronomy is over my head (and yours too), but I know how to find answers. The first way is to observe and study to build up a mental database. The second way is to look something up in a book or online.

If you see a solid bright light or object in the sky, night after night, in just about the same position, it's a planet or a star. A comet would appear the same way, except it would be fuzzy with a faint tail. Stars twinkle, while planets generally do not.

What if you see something streak through the sky in a straight line, for only a few seconds, brighter than any star or planet? That would be a meteor—most often a tiny fragment of rock that enters the Earth's atmosphere and then burns up due to friction. Most don't reach the ground. A meteor may seem to be just a few miles away, but in reality, it could be hundreds of miles away. Most meteors do not make any sound, although the large ones can create an explosion. Meteors happen day and night, worldwide, randomly. It's hard to notice a meteor that happens in the day. They are too tiny and brief to be seen.

Astronomers call meteors fireballs. To see how many people report seeing fireballs, or to report seeing one, go to the website of the American Meteor Society—not to be confused with the American Meteorological Society!

Meteors do become more numerous during one of the many annual meteor showers. Late fall gives more opportunities to see them because nights are long and Earth's orbit takes it through clouds of dust and tiny rocks, to create meteor showers. All increase the odds of spotting a meteor if you are a stargazer. While a meteor is often nicknamed a shooting star or falling star, those are very misleading monikers. Stars don't fall, except in Hollywood.

What people call a shooting star is a meteor. On the other hand, the sun is a star. Can you imagine what would happen if something the size of the sun were to rush through our solar system?! The gravitational disruption would be the end of the neat orbits that we and our neighboring planets have. For us, on Earth, it would truly be the end.

The meteors that make news are the ones that often hit the ground and are found. Those are called meteorites. Those could range in size from that of a baseball, to that of a bus. The huge majority of meteors are closer to something between the size of a pebble and a grain of sand. When you consider that Earth is covered mostly by ocean, that immediately tells you that two thirds of meteorites end up like an errant golf drive—in the water.

For just about any meteor shower, put your attention on the darkest part of the sky. Most meteor showers are most active after midnight. There's never a guarantee that you'll see much, in part because you can only view a portion of the sky at one time. Meteors will happen that you miss! Some people may have an expectation that a meteor shower is a constant barrage of meteors. There are historical accounts of extraordinary rains of meteors, like those on November 12, 1833, in which people compared the meteors to fireworks, but were also frightened because they had never known of such a display. Even in the very active meteor showers, if you see one meteor every 5 or 10 minutes, you would be lucky.

For many of us city slickers, light pollution makes it much more difficult to spot the heavens in detail. Get to the outskirts, the country, or a coastal beach if you can. Regardless of where you are, go outside, and let your eyes adjust to the darkness. Don't look at your mobile device because your eyes will have to readjust to darkness!

If you see a small solid white light, silently gliding across the sky within a couple of hours after sunset or a couple hours before sunrise, then it's a satellite or the International Space Station. There are thousands of satellites orbiting Earth. They reflect light from the sun back to our eyes because they are so high above the ground, in space. There are clusters of internet satellites that when launched, appear as a string or train of lights for several days or weeks, before they separate into their final orbits, widely spaced apart. The Space Station is typically the brightest solid dot you'll see, because it is much bigger than satellites.

If you see a cluster of objects, travelling as a group, where some decelerate, and all are leaving trails, that could be old satellite debris entering the atmosphere and burning up. Another object that will leave a fire trail is the re-entry vehicle for Space Station astronauts.

If you see a solid light, accompanied by flashing lights, and/or you hear an engine, that's an airplane or helicopter!

Now, what I can't identify or figure out is when people tell me a light is moving erratically or changing colors or moving in formation with other lights. Video that people share is often shaky and blurry, with no reference for altitude or speed. I never know if it's zoomed in or ultra-wide. I can only guess military aircraft, drones, weather or research balloons, searchlights or laser lights, Chinese lanterns, or someone playing a hoax. I get the sense that some people want me to tell them that it's an otherworldly UFO that has entered our airspace. I've never known of a spacecraft coming to Earth that didn't start on Earth. If it ever happens, I'm not the one to ask! By the way, UFO simply means an object that is flying and unidentified. It doesn't necessarily mean it comes from another planet.

Final Thoughts

In one of my job transitions, upon letting my TV station management know I was not going to renew my contract, I was asked, "What will you miss most about not working here?" I paused, laughed, and answered, "The paycheck." Over time, the TV industry and weather broadcasting have changed. In some ways good, in other ways not so good. I've changed, too, but I wouldn't trade or change any of my past moves, and decisions, because each one propelled me forward in a field that I love, and allowed me to be part of my community, helping others, being a mentor, a role model, meeting people who have become dear friends like family, and earning a healthy salary through persistence and effort.

TV was a huge part of my life, but it now is literally a previous chapter. The things I liked most about it, educating about weather and serving the public through public outreach, I still do. I just do them less frequently, now on my terms. Throughout my career, I estimate I made nearly 800 school visits (sometimes returning to the same schools), reaching over 80,000 kids. I spoke at luncheons, banquets, fundraisers and other events for adults over 350 times. On TV, I appeared in over 22,000 newscasts! I estimate that I spoke a total of at least 100,000 minutes, unscripted. That would be 10 weeks of non-stop talking!! I wonder how many times I said, "partly cloudy"?

What's funny to me is now that I'm out in public in regular street clothes, many people have a hard time placing where they think they know me from! Those that do recognize me occasionally call me by my former co-anchors' or reporters' names. I still respond. There was one man who came up to me and called me by another anchor's name. I was just about to correct him, until he asked for money! I declined to help him, so I guess he's cursing my old anchor. Some people say that they still watch me on TV. Either they are being polite, or I really burned an impression into their mind!

One of the factors in my TV retirement decision was to go out on top, not when I began to decline. I didn't want to be the guy on TV of whom people remark, "when is he going to retire?!" I've seen too many athletes, entertainers, and politicians try to hold onto the glory and celebrity they once had, when they were past their prime. In any endeavor, you have to know when it's time to go.

I'm definitely satisfied and pleased with my TV career. Aside from where I worked, I interviewed at WKYC-TV in Cleveland, and at WXIA-TV in Atlanta. After I got to WGN in Chicago and was looking to move on in the middle 1990s, I interviewed at WXYZ-TV in Detroit, WDAF-TV in Kansas City, and WBRC-TV in Birmingham. I think back to how different my career and life could have been if I had gone to any of those stations. Different does not necessarily mean better! You can spend your life wondering, "what if?" but you will never know. Accept the path you have taken and make it the best it can be. You can always change the path but that does not guarantee the trajectory you hope for.

In my TV career "afterlife," many people suggest things I can do in retirement. I nod my head and smile when people do that. They think that I am bored and have nothing but free time. No, I have many hobbies, projects and endeavors to keep me busy. I immediately said "no" when asked to run for a political office. The politician who asked said that the public trusts me and I would be one of the few politicians with a science background, and that's true. I didn't retire from TV to take a new job with a higher workload. I have no interest in being a politician. It's an endeavor where you cannot please everyone, and more often you can't be successful because of... politics! That was the second time in my life that someone genuinely suggested I run for political office.

Right after retirement, I was invited to run for President of the American Meteorological Society. That is the largest organization of professional meteorologists in the United States. I ran and I was elected. That made me the second person to be elected president of the National Weather Association and then the American Meteorological Society. These are not things I ever imagined I'd do. In fact, for most of my roles and achievements within my professional organizations, they happened because someone asked me if I was willing to step up.

I no longer have the stress of monitoring and covering severe weather. I'll admit that I periodically have a dream that I'm still on TV. The dream is never the kind where I wish I was back, though. Sometimes the dream becomes a nightmare, similar to ones I had when I was working, and that was that some technical issue prevented me from delivering the weather segment on TV.

Do I watch local meteorologists now in weather threats? Generally, no. The main reason is that I follow the weather closely enough as a meteorologist, using raw data that tells me what I need to know. A smaller reason is that I get distracted by the presentation and find myself saying, "I wouldn't have done it that way!" Should you follow local meteorologists in weather threats? Definitely, yes.

I'm also distracted by multiple sponsor logos in the weather segment along with words scrolling across the bottom of the screen. Station branding and slogans are added to create more visual clutter. These block data and graphics. Even worse is when the meteorologist has to verbalize the name of a sponsor, taking away from the spoken message. These things are so common that most people don't notice, but just imagine if you were reading the story of Little Red Riding Hood to children, or teaching a college class, or delivering a sermon, and in the middle of it you pause to include the name and logo of a sponsor!

What about local news? Do I watch? Yes, I randomly choose different stations each time to get different perspectives. Having worked in TV news for decades, I get distracted by the promotions, and sponsors, and the rhythm that most local newscasts follow in how they order their stories. As new generations of producers and reporters rotate in and out of local TV stations, the writing language remains largely the same. How many times have you heard a news report after a tornado that said something like "residents are picking up the pieces after a twister left a trail of destruction, tossing cars like toys and snapping trees like toothpicks"?

Do I watch national news? Yes. That was always a part of my life, given my generation. I know that network TV national news should be giving me the most essential information that I need, in 30 minutes (minus many minutes of commercials for medications). I spend more time reading news online from reputable sources. Regardless of the formula approach of many news outlets, journalism is a noble and necessary profession to educate and inform the public, and that certainly includes weather journalism in the form of daily weather forecasts.

The TV news industry continues to morph, but it is not dead. The use of Artificial Intelligence will have impact, but it can't replace the first-hand and generational knowledge broadcasters have of their communities, nor can it replace the communication conventions of eye contact and the human emotions of concern, compassion, empathy, fear, joy and pain.

My career as a TV meteorologist was a joy. Through the years, I always got a big laugh hearing how my young nieces and nephews one day stumbled upon my work and exclaimed to their parents, "Uncle Alan is on TV!"

Being on TV and social media didn't make me who I am. It's what I did.

About the Author

How many meteorologists have ever gone viral for doing something positive? Not many, but Alan Sealls did! He was proclaimed "Best Weatherman Ever" by "the internet" in 2017 for his concise, coherent, enlightening, and informative forecasts of Hurricane Irma, viewed millions of times around the world. That was no surprise to people who watched him on TV over his lengthy career, taking him to Milwaukee, Chicago, and then to Mobile as a chief meteorologist, with work at WGN and at CNN.

Alan is also an adjunct college professor. Dozens of his students are weather broadcasters around the United States. Alan Sealls earned meteorology degrees from Cornell University and from Florida State University. He was elected president of the National Weather Association, and then the American Meteorological Society (AMS). He is a Fellow of the AMS too. He holds broadcast certifications from both of those organizations. With more than a dozen Emmy awards, and more than two dozen national, state, and local awards, Alan has always aimed for excellence in science communication. Tens of thousands of children and adults have witnessed that in his public presentations. In addition to providing weather safety seminars to businesses, Alan is frequently invited to speak at universities and at national conferences, and he is often retained by attorneys as a consulting meteorologist or expert witness in legal cases where weather is a factor.

Alan is also an accomplished weather photographer. His weather photos and video work have been used in textbooks, magazines, newspapers, science journals, documentaries, and on network TV programs.

Find Alan Sealls on social media and at alansealls.com

Other books by author

Weather Things in Photos

Weather Things you Always Wanted to Know

www.ingramcontent.com/pod-product-compliance
Lightning Source LLC
Chambersburg PA
CBHW021612120626
46545CB00001B/183